"If you love Luke's Gospel, which exalts Jesus and shows him as the fulfillment of the Old Testament, you will love this treatment of Luke's message.
Full of insight and sensitive to Luke's own hermeneutic of the wider message
of Scripture, this book is a treasure."

Craig S. Keener, F. M. and Ada Thompson Professor of Biblical
Studies, Asbury Theological Seminary

"Open up Luke anew with the help of this fresh and faithful tour from a
knowledgeable guide. Adam, the exodus, the wilderness, angels and demons,
the Son of Man—it's all there in the Gospel of Luke. Gladd considers these
topics, and more, to help us see the rich Old Testament contours of our great
Savior and his great work on our behalf."

Brandon D. Crowe, Professor of New Testament, Westminster
Theological Seminary

"The length, breadth, and depth of Luke's Gospel can be daunting. Blending
careful exegesis, theological synthesis, and canonical sensitivity, Benjamin
Gladd provides an accessible and faithful exploration of some of its most
significant themes, paying particular attention to their Old Testament roots.
This book is ideal for enhancing one's personal study, preparing to preach
or teach, or even as a supplemental textbook in a class on Luke. Highly
recommended!"

Matthew S. Harmon, Professor of New Testament Studies, Grace
College and Theological Seminary; author, *Asking the Right Questions:
A Practical Guide to Understanding and Applying the Bible*

"*From the Manger to the Throne* is required reading for students of Luke's
Gospel! Benjamin Gladd ably guides readers to see how Jesus fulfills Old
Testament expectations as true Israel, the long-awaited messianic king, the
incarnate Lord, and more, leading us to greater confidence in Christ and joyful
participation in his kingdom."

Brian J. Tabb, Academic Dean and Professor of Biblical Studies,
Bethlehem College and Seminary

T0334763

"The Third Gospel takes us from incarnation to ascension, or as Benjamin Gladd puts it, from the manger to the throne. We need to take this journey with Luke so that we might hear and rejoice in the good news—with Mary in her humble estate, with shepherds in a field, with tax collectors and sinners at meals, with Zacchaeus in a tree, and with the penitent criminal on the cross. Gladd discerns major themes and motifs to help us get our bearings, and he is a faithful guide who has insights to share and Old Testament connections to disclose. The theology of Luke's Gospel ultimately reveals the person and work of Christ to us. Gladd's work is clear, accessible, and edifying. Read it not only to understand more about Luke's Gospel but also to join the angels in celebrating good news of great joy for all people."

Mitchell L. Chase, Preaching Pastor, Kosmosdale Baptist Church, Louisville, Kentucky; Associate Professor of Biblical Studies, The Southern Baptist Theological Seminary

"Benjamin Gladd has provided a rich resource for readers of Luke's Gospel. Following the lead of Luke, and Jesus himself, Gladd shows that the patterns and promises of the whole of Scripture enrich our appreciation and understanding of the saving rule of the Lord Jesus. An expert guide who knows and loves his subject, Gladd deepens our understanding of who Jesus is and what he accomplished with a stimulating investigation into how Luke's portrait of the Lord Jesus is tied to the Old Testament. Fresh insights abound. By God's grace, the end result for readers of this volume will be, like the disciples at the end of Luke's Gospel, joyful worship of the Lord Jesus."

Alan J. Thompson, Head of New Testament Department, Sydney Missionary and Bible College, Australia

"This deft and insightful thematic reading of Luke's Gospel majors on Jesus, the Old Testament, and fulfillments of the latter by the former. But Gladd extends the sweep of God's work from creation and the fall, through Jesus, to the church across the centuries, and into the age to come. If there is a richer, better informed, and more concise biblical-theological reading of the Third Gospel, I have not come across it. Students, pastors, and scholars alike will profit immensely."

Robert W. Yarbrough, Professor of New Testament, Covenant Theological Seminary

From the Manger to the Throne

New Testament Theology

Edited by Thomas R. Schreiner and Brian S. Rosner

From the Manger
to the Throne

A Theology of Luke

Benjamin L. Gladd

CROSSWAY®

WHEATON, ILLINOIS

Cover design: Kevin Lipp

First printing 2022

Printed in the United States of America

Trade paperback ISBN: 978–1–4335–7523–5

ePub ISBN: 978-1-4335-7526-6

PDF ISBN: 978-1-4335-7524-2

Mobipocket ISBN: 978-1-4335-7525-9

Library of Congress Cataloging-in-Publication Data

Names: Gladd, Benjamin L., author.

Title: From the manger to the throne : a theology of Luke / Benjamin L. Gladd.

Description: Wheaton, Illinois : Crossway, 2022. | Series: New Testament theology | Includes bibliographical references and index.

Identifiers: LCCN 2021059387 (print) | LCCN 2021059388 (ebook) | ISBN 9781433575235 (trade paperback) | ISBN 9781433575242 (pdf) | ISBN 9781433575259 (mobipocket) | ISBN 9781433575266 (epub)

Subjects: LCSH: Bible. Luke—Theology.

Classification: LCC BS2595.52 .G56 2022 (print) | LCC BS2595.52 (ebook) | DDC 226.4/06—dc23/eng/20220224

LC record available at https://lccn.loc.gov/2021059387

LC ebook record available at https://lccn.loc.gov/2021059388

Crossway is a publishing ministry of Good News Publishers.

VP		31		30		29		28		27		26		25		24		23		22
15	14	13	12	11	10	9	8	7	6	5	4	3	2	1				

Contents

Tables

Series Preface

THERE ARE REMARKABLY FEW TREATMENTS of the big ideas of single books of the New Testament. Readers can find brief coverage in Bible dictionaries, in some commentaries, and in New Testament theologies, but such books are filled with other information and are not devoted to unpacking the theology of each New Testament book in its own right. Technical works concentrating on various themes of New Testament theology often have a narrow focus, treating some aspect of the teaching of, say, Matthew or Hebrews in isolation from the rest of the book's theology.

The New Testament Theology series seeks to fill this gap by providing students of Scripture with readable book-length treatments of the distinctive teaching of each New Testament book or collection of books. The volumes approach the text from the perspective of biblical theology. They pay due attention to the historical and literary dimensions of the text, but their main focus is on presenting the teaching of particular New Testament books about God and his relations to the world on their own terms, maintaining sight of the Bible's overarching narrative and Christocentric focus. Such biblical theology is of fundamental importance to biblical and expository preaching and informs exegesis, systematic theology, and Christian ethics.

The twenty volumes in the series supply comprehensive, scholarly, and accessible treatments of theological themes from an evangelical perspective. We envision them being of value to students, preachers, and interested laypeople. When preparing an expository sermon series, for example, pastors can find a healthy supply of informative commentaries, but there are few options for coming to terms with the overall teaching of each book of the New Testament. As well as being useful in sermon and Bible study preparation, the volumes will also be of value as textbooks in college and seminary exegesis classes. Our prayer is that they contribute to a deeper understanding of and commitment to the kingdom and glory of God in Christ.

Writing a brief theology of one of the four Gospels is daunting, and perhaps Luke is particularly challenging since it is the longest of the four. Ben Gladd approaches the theology of the Gospel of Luke from a fascinating vantage point. He particularly considers what the Gospel has to say about Jesus Christ and the fulfillment of the Old Testament. It is virtually impossible to cover everything Luke teaches in his Gospel, but all readers will agree that the Lukan story centers on Jesus. Readers might be tempted to think that a relatively short study that focuses on Jesus will be superficial. They will see, however, that Gladd mines the Old Testament to give us an in-depth and profound portrait of the Christ in the Lukan account. We find, then, a theology of Luke's Gospel that is both accessible and profound, one where the roots of Luke's theology are unpacked and explored. If we can borrow the language of Matthew (Matt. 13:52), readers will find many treasures, both new and old.

Thomas R. Schreiner and Brian S. Rosner

Preface

WILLIAM FAULKNER IS REPORTED TO have compared writing a book to "building a chicken coop in a high wind. You grab any board or shingle flying by or loose on the ground and nail it down fast."[1] This metaphor resonated with me as I wrote this short volume on one of the most brilliant documents ever written. The Third Gospel is roughly 19,483 words in Greek, the longest book in the New Testament, and not one word is wasted.

I'm thankful for Tom Schreiner and Brian Rosner asking me to write this volume on Luke. Their editorial comments strengthened the manuscript. I've admired both of these men for a long time, having read their works since graduate school, so I'm honored to participate in this series. I had recently completed my *Handbook on the Gospels* (Baker Academic, 2021) when they asked if I would consider contributing to Crossway's New Testament Theology series. This project allowed me to return to Luke's Gospel again and discover anew his presentation of Jesus.

Writing a theology of any biblical book is a tricky endeavor, especially a theology of a Gospel. To a great degree, each Gospel covers the same ground and announces the good news of Christ's substitutionary life, death, and resurrection. The Jesus of Matthew is the same Jesus of John. Jesus is Israel's divine Lord and her long-awaited messianic king,

---

1 This quotation is often repeated and attributed to Faulkner, but I am unable to identify its source.

who inaugurates the eschatological kingdom. Those who trust in Jesus receive the forgiveness of sins and gain entrance into the new creation, and those who do not trust in him bear God's curse and spend eternity in eternal torment. But each Gospel also presents Jesus in a unique way. We have four Gospels for a reason.

This project is subtitled "*A Theology of Luke.*" It does not endeavor to be *the* theology of Luke and integrate all aspects of the Third Gospel. Instead, this volume attempts to get at the heart of Luke's message by sketching some of his main ideas and showing how they intersect with one another. I also attempt to carve out the Old Testament's presentation of each theme and then relate how those themes flourish in Jesus of Nazareth.

The Gospel of Luke is part of a two-volume work, as it was published alongside the book of Acts. What Jesus accomplished in the Third Gospel is proclaimed in the book of Acts, and the themes Luke establishes in his Gospel are unfurled in the book of Acts. Luke-Acts, then, should be read as a whole. By narrowly focusing on only his Gospel, I am, in some sense, cutting against the grain. I try to keep an eye on Acts as I unpack Luke's Gospel, but I recommend that readers pick up the Acts volume in the New Testament Theology series and discover how Luke finishes the story.

Personally, this was a difficult book to write. Yes, Luke's Gospel is challenging in its own right, but this project was especially difficult because of what transpired in my life. On Thanksgiving of 2020, our house caught fire, and the damage was extensive. We lost everything. Thankfully, no one was injured. A few months later, in the spring of 2021, I lost my father to a long battle with cancer. He was bigger than life, and anyone who met him never forgot him. Thankfully, too, he is in heaven worshiping the Lamb. Penning this book in the midst of these two life-changing events proved overwhelming at times. Writing a book requires a great deal of emotional and creative bandwidth, and I often sat down to write with nothing left in the tank. But my soul was nourished as I drank from the life-giving well of Luke's Gospel.

Benjamin L. Gladd
January 2022

Abbreviations

1 En.	1 Enoch
2 En.	2 Enoch
1 Esd.	1 Esdras
1QM	War Scroll
2 Bar.	2 Baruch
4 Macc.	4 Maccabees
Ag. Ap.	*Against Apion*, by Josephus
Ant.	*Jewish Antiquities*, by Josephus
BBR	*Bulletin for Biblical Research*
BDAG	Frederick W. Danker, Walter Bauer, William F. Arndt, and F. Wilbur Gingrich. *Greek-English Lexicon of the New Testament and Other Early Christian Literature.* 3rd ed. Chicago: University of Chicago Press, 2000
BECNT	Baker Exegetical Commentary on the New Testament
Brenton	Sir Lancelot Brenton's translation of the Septuagint
BZNW	Beihefte zur Zeitschrift für die neutestamentliche Wissenschaft
CD	Damascus Document
Creation	*On the Creation of the World*, by Philo
EGGNT	Exegetical Guide to the Greek New Testament
ESBT	Essential Studies in Biblical Theology
Ezek. Trag.	Ezekiel the Tragedian
Gk.	Greek

Heb.	Hebrew
JSNTSup	Journal for the Study of the New Testament Supplement Series
Jub.	Jubilees
J. W.	*Jewish War*, by Josephus
LAE	Life of Adam and Eve
Let. Aris.	Letter of Aristeas
LHBOTS	Library of Hebrew Bible/Old Testament Studies
m. Ned.	Mishnah Nedarim
Moses	*On the Life of Moses*, by Philo
LNTS	Library of New Testament Studies
LXX	Septuagint
LXX-Theo	Theodotion's Septuagint
Mart. Isa.	Martyrdom and Ascension of Isaiah
Migration	*On the Migration of Abraham*, by Philo
MT	Masoretic Text
NICNT	New International Commentary on the New Testament
NICOT	New International Commentary on the Old Testament
NIGTC	New International Greek Testament Commentary
NIVAC	NIV Application Commentary
NSBT	New Studies in Biblical Theology
OG	Old Greek (Septuagint)
OTL	Old Testament Library
PNTC	Pillar New Testament Commentary
Pss. Sol.	Psalms of Solomon
RB	*Revue Biblique*
Rev. Ezra	Revelation of Ezra
Sir.	Sirach
Sus.	Susanna
T. Benj.	Testament of Benjamin
T. Lev.	Testament of Levi

Tob.	Tobit
WBC	Word Biblical Commentary
WUNT	Wissenschaftliche Untersuchungen zum Neuen Testament
ZECNT	Zondervan Exegetical Commentary on the New Testament

Introduction

NOT ALL NEW TESTAMENT BOOKS CONTAIN purpose statements, so when we come across them we should pay close attention. Fortunately, Luke delivers his purpose statement in the prologue: "It seemed good to me . . . to write an orderly account for you, most excellent Theophilus, that *you may have certainty concerning the things you have been taught*" (Luke 1:3–4).[1] "Most excellent Theophilus" is an enigmatic figure, as he's only mentioned here and in Acts 1:1. It is possible, if not likely, that he is the patron of Luke-Acts, since writing in the ancient world was financially burdensome, especially for a document as large as the Third Gospel. The phrase "most excellent" may also indicate that Theophilus is a prominent official (see Acts 23:26; 24:3; 26:25).[2] The name Theophilus means "lover of God," which may connote that he's a God-fearing Gentile. Theophilus appears to have embraced the Israelite faith and Scriptures and, subsequently, placed his faith in the risen Christ. Though Luke mentions only one individual in the prologue, a wider audience is certainly in view. Since Luke the Evangelist, most likely a Gentile himself, focuses on the incorporation of Gentiles in Luke-Acts, Luke's audience is probably Gentile Christians to a large extent.

The "things" that Theophilus learned (Luke 1:1) likely refer to the other literary accounts of Jesus's life, and the description that these

---

1 See similarly Josephus, *Ag. Ap.* 1.1–3, 2.1–2.
2 See also Josephus, *Ant.* 18.273; 20.12; Philo, *Moses* 430; Ezek. Trag. 243.

things "have been accomplished" stresses the fulfillment of Israel's Scriptures. To summarize, Theophilus appears to have learned about the broad contours of Jesus's life, death, and resurrection, so Luke writes his Gospel to affirm the truthfulness of these events that fulfill Old Testament expectations and that have been communicated by apostolic eyewitnesses (see Acts 1:3, 21–22).

This introduction sets the stage for the remainder of this project. My aim here is to sketch an overview of Luke's Gospel and trace some of the more significant uses of the Old Testament at each major juncture.[3] There are more than thirty explicit Old Testament quotations and several hundred allusions.[4] The result of this investigation should give us a better grasp of Luke's narrative and a deeper appreciation for *how* the Third Gospel appropriates the Old Testament in the life of Christ.

Jesus's Birth and Baptism (1:5–3:38)

After the prologue of Luke 1:1–4, the Third Gospel transitions into an account about John the Baptist's parents, Zechariah and Elizabeth (1:5–25). Whereas Matthew's account focuses on Mary and Joseph (Matt. 1:18–24), Luke informs his readers about the birth of Jesus's cousin John. The narrative first highlights Zechariah, a priest, ministering in the temple where the angel Gabriel informs him that his wife Elizabeth will give birth to a son, who will be called John (Luke 1:13).

---

3   For treatments on Luke's use of the Old Testament, see, for example, David W. Pao and Eckhard J. Schnabel, "Luke," in *Commentary on the New Testament Use of the Old Testament*, ed. G. K. Beale and D. A. Carson (Grand Rapids, MI: Baker Academic, 2007), 251–415; D. L. Bock, *Proclamation from Prophecy and Pattern: Lucan Old Testament Christology*, JSNTSup 12 (Sheffield: Sheffield Academic Press, 1987); Craig A. Evans and J. A. Sanders, eds., *Luke and Scripture: The Function of Sacred Tradition in Luke-Acts* (Minneapolis: Fortress, 1993); Roger Stronstad, *The Charismatic Theology of St. Luke: Trajectories from the Old Testament to Luke-Acts*, 2nd ed. (Grand Rapids, MI: Baker Academic, 2012); C. A. Kimball, *Jesus's Exposition of the Old Testament in Luke's Gospel*, JSNTSup 94 (Sheffield: Sheffield Academic Press, 1994).

4   David W. Pao, "Luke, Book of," in *Dictionary of the New Testament Use of the Old Testament*, ed. G. K. Beale, D. A. Carson, Benjamin L. Gladd, and Andrew D. Naselli (Grand Rapids, MI: Baker Academic, forthcoming).

Zechariah, though, remains incredulous because he is "an old man" and his wife is "advanced in years" (1:18).

Six month's into Elizabeth's pregnancy, Gabriel makes a second visit but this time to Mary (1:26). He promises Mary, a virgin, that she will "bear a son" and that she "shall call his name Jesus" (1:31). On the whole, Luke 1–2 compares and contrasts the birth of John with the birth of Jesus. While John the Baptist is great, Jesus is greater in every way. The virgin birth (1:34) and the appellations "Son of the Most High" (1:32) and the "Son of God" (1:35) clearly affirm Jesus's divinity and preexistence. A few sentences later, Elizabeth calls Jesus "my Lord" (*kyriou mou*; 1:43). The term *Lord* (*kyrios*) has occurred ten times in the narrative so far, and each occurrence refers to Israel's God (e.g., 1:6, 16, 32). In Elizabeth's confession that Jesus is her "Lord," Luke thoughtfully identifies Jesus as Israel's Lord incarnate.[5] Luke 1:45 confirms this observation when Elizabeth declares, "Blessed is she [Mary] who believed that there would be a fulfillment of what was spoken to her from *the Lord* [*kyrios*]" (cf. 1:38).

Mary's prayer, known as the Magnificat (1:46–55), makes an incredible amount of contact with the Old Testament. Prominent in this regard is Hannah's well-known prayer of thanksgiving in 1 Samuel 2:1–10, where Hannah thanks God for giving her a child. The overall point of Hannah's prayer is that God will destroy the proud but will raise up the humble (1 Sam. 2:4–10a) and that he will "give strength to his king [David?] and exalt the horn of his anointed" (1 Sam. 2:10b). Mary appears to be aware of Hannah's famous prayer as she asserts that

He has shown strength with his arm;
  he has scattered the proud in the thoughts of their hearts;
he has brought down the mighty from their thrones
  and exalted those of humble estate. (Luke 1:51–52)

---

5 James Edwards comments on 1:43, "What is conceived in Mary's womb can be described only in the language proper to Israel's unique and incomparable God" (*The Gospel according to Luke*, PNTC [Grand Rapids, MI: Eerdmans, 2015], 53). See also the discussion in C. Kavin Rowe, *Early Narrative Christology: The Lord in the Gospel of Luke*, BZNW 139 (New York: de Gruyter, 2006), 48–49.

Mary not only recalls Hannah's prayer but also alludes to several Old Testament texts that refer to the first exodus. God possessing "strength with his arm," for example, recalls texts such Isaiah 51:9:

> Awake, awake, *put on strength,*
>> *O arm of the* LORD;
> awake, as in days of old,
>> the generations of long ago,
> Was it not you who cut Rahab in pieces,
>> who pierced the dragon? (see also LXX Ex. 6:1; 32:11; Isa. 40:10; 63:12)

The scattering of God's enemies (Luke 1:51) also brings the exodus to mind (see LXX Num 10:34). Mary, then, believes that God will bring down all forms of rule—physical and spiritual—through King Jesus and that he will powerfully redeem his people in the second exodus (see discussion in chapter 1).

Luke then recounts the birth of John (1:57–66) and Zechariah's hymn of response, the Benedictus (1:68–79). Zechariah explicitly connects the forthcoming birth of Jesus with God who "raised up a horn of salvation . . . in the house of his servant David, *as he spoke by the mouth of his holy prophets from of old*" (1:69–70). While Luke doesn't disclose what Old Testament texts are in mind here, we can nearly be certain that popular texts from such books as 2 Samuel and Ezekiel are in view. In the same breath, Zechariah also invokes the Abrahamic covenant (Luke 1:73–75; see, e.g., Gen. 12:1–9; 15:4–20; 17:4–22). Baby Jesus, then, inaugurates not only the Davidic covenant—that David's son would secure the throne and establish peace throughout the empire—but also the Abrahamic covenant. The time has come for Israel to be a light to the nations so that they may behold the face of God in the promised land (Ex. 19:6).

Jesus is born in Bethlehem, "the city of David" (Luke 2:4–7). Following the birth, Joseph and Mary take their baby to the temple, where Simeon prophesies over him. At the end of his prophetic hymn, the Nunc Dimittis, Simeon exclaims to God that Jesus will be

> a light for revelation to the Gentiles,
>> and for glory to your people Israel. (2:32)

He partially quotes Isaiah 49:6 and explicitly tethers Jesus to the long-awaited promise of redemption. Isaiah predicted that God would raise up a single individual who is *the* faithful one of God, true Israel. This faithful servant stimulates faith among unbelieving Israelites and forges a remnant within the nation. The servant, then, will also bring the nations into the covenant community (Isa. 42:1–9; 49:1–6; 50:4–9; 52:13–53:12).

After Luke narrates the account of the twelve-year-old Jesus baffling Israel's leaders at the temple (2:41–52), John the Baptist begins his career, announcing the "baptism of repentance" (3:3). Luke then cites the famous text from Isaiah 40:3–5. The thrust of the quotation is that the time has now arrived for Yahweh to redeem his people from spiritual captivity through his faithful servant Jesus. God has begun to cut a pathway in the desert for his people to travel to the new creation. The last line of the quotation, "and all flesh shall see the salvation of God" (3:6), uniquely underscores Jesus's concern to bring the nations into fellowship with the covenant community.

Following Jesus's baptism, where God declared Jesus to be his "beloved Son" (3:21–23; see Ps. 2:7; Isa. 42:1), Luke lists Jesus's genealogy (3:23–38). Beginning with Joseph and tracing his lineage all the way back to Seth and Adam, Luke presents Jesus not simply as a descendant of the patriarch Abraham (3:34) and of King David (3:31) but also of the progenitor of humanity—Adam himself (3:38). The explicit connection between Jesus and Adam is of no small consequence.[6]

To review, Luke explicitly identifies Jesus as the long-awaited descendant of David, Yahweh himself, Isaiah's faithful servant, and the

---

6   John Nolland, *Luke 1–9:20*, WBC (Grand Rapids, MI: Zondervan, 1989), 173, rightly sees the importance of this connection. He avers, "Luke would have us see that Jesus takes his place in the human family and thus in its (since Adam's disobedience) flawed sonship; however, in his own person, in virtue of his unique origin (Luke 1:35) but also as worked out in his active obedience (4:1–13), he marks a new beginning to sonship and sets it on an entirely new footing."

second Adam. That Jesus is simultaneously Israel's God incarnate (the "Lord") *and* faithful Adam is critical. Jesus is the God-man, and both natures fulfill different aspects of the Old Testament.

Jesus's Wilderness Temptation and Galilean Ministry (4:1–9:50)

The first three chapters introduce Luke's readers to the person of Jesus and how he relates to Old Testament promises. Beginning in Luke 4, the readers begin to see *how* these promises are fleshed out. For example, Jesus is clearly the long-awaited Messiah who is expected to defeat Israel's enemies (1:32–33; 2:4, 11; 3:22), but in Luke 4 we begin to see how that messianic reign is executed.

Old Testament and Jewish expectations of a coming Messiah are as diverse as they are widespread. The common denominator among these expectations, though, is that the Messiah was expected to descend from David, establish God's eternal rule on the earth, and subdue Israel's enemies.[7] The Messiah would be the catalyst in ushering the new age, the age of righteousness, on the earth. Jesus's first act of business as Israel's King is waging war in the wilderness against the devil. On the one hand, isn't this what we should expect from Israel's King? Isn't Jesus supposed to battle Israel's enemies right out of the gate? Yes. But what makes Jesus's fulfillment of the Old Testament odd is how he does so. He brandishes not a sword of steel but the very Word of God. He does not lead a rebellion against Rome but battles Satan himself. In other words, Jesus fulfills Old Testament messianic expectations primarily *on a cosmic, spiritual level.*

Jesus cites the book of Deuteronomy three times during the wilderness temptation (Deut. 8:3 in Luke 4:4; Deut. 6:13 in Luke 4:8; Deut. 6:16 in Luke 4:12). Each of these quotations likely hinges

---

7   See, e.g., Gen. 3:15; 49:8–10; Num, 24:17; 2 Sam. 7; Pss. 2; 78; 89; 110; 132; Isa. 9:6–7; 11:1–5; 53; Dan. 7:13–14; 9:25–26; Pss. Sol. 17.21–46; 2 Bar. 30.1–5a; 40.1–2; T. Lev. 18:1–9; CD-A XII, 23; CD-B XIX, 10; XX, 1; 4Q161 8–10 III, 18–22. For a helpful, balanced survey of the Messiah in Second Temple Judaism, see Kenneth E. Pomykala, "Messianism," in *The Eerdmans Dictionary of Early Judaism*, ed. John J. Collins and Daniel C. Harlow (Grand Rapids, MI: Eerdmans, 2010), 938–42.

on a typological correspondence between Jesus and the nation of Israel. The nation's failure anticipates his success. Jesus isn't the only one who fights with Scripture though. The devil alludes to Daniel 7:14 in the second temptation and then explicitly quotes Psalm 91:11–12 in the third temptation. On both accounts, however, the devil abuses the meaning of the Old Testament (see discussion in chapters 5 and 6).

Having initially and decisively conquered the devil, Jesus ventures to Nazareth where he reads from Isaiah 61:1–2 in the local synagogue. He even claims that Isaiah 61 is "fulfilled in your [the Nazarenes'] hearing" (Luke 4:21), announcing the arrival of the eschatological year of jubilee and the descent of glory (see discussion in chapter 7). Now is the time for *all* of God's people—rich and poor, male and female, Jew and Gentile, popular and outcast—to enjoy the Lord. Ironically, Jesus's longtime friends utterly reject him (4:23). Following in the footsteps of the idolatrous Israelites who rebuffed Elijah and Elisha, these Nazarenes denounce Jesus. But their rejection paves the way for Gentile acceptance: just like the widow of Zarephath and Naaman the Syrian believed the prophetic word (4:24–30), the nations will eagerly follow the Son of Man.

The narrative picks up steam. In Galilee, Jesus begins his itinerant ministry of visiting synagogues and performing miracles and exorcisms (4:31–44). Jesus performs approximately twenty-one miracles in the Third Gospel.[8] These events concretely demonstrate the in-breaking of the kingdom and the establishment of the new age. Jesus calls his first crop of disciples (5:1–11) and declares the forgiveness of a paralytic's sins (5:17–26). Jesus then enjoys a "great feast" at a tax collector's house (5:27–32). This banquet with tax collectors and sinners is highly reminiscent of Isaiah 25:6, where God organizes "for all peoples a feast of rich food." Table fellowship, so prominent in Luke's Gospel (7:36–50; 10:38–42; 11:37–54; 14:1–24; 15:1–32; 19:1–10;

---

8 Luke 4:31–37, 38–41; 5:12–16, 17–26; 6:6–11, 17–19; 7:1–10, 11–17; 8:22–25, 26–39, 40–56; 9:10–17, 37–42; 13:10–17; 14:1–24; 17:12–19; 18:35–43; 22:47–53; 24:12.

24:13–35), must be interpreted through the lens of Isaiah's prophecy.[9] The Old Testament yearned for the day when Yahweh would dwell in the midst of his people and nourish them with his presence (see Ps. 63:5; Rev. 19:9). Strikingly, Jesus, the Lord incarnate, is the one who dines with the outsiders, the tax collectors and sinners.

The Jewish leaders soon take notice of Jesus's actions. Forgiving the sins of the paralytic (5:17–26) and eating an intimate meal with unclean outsiders (5:27–32) draw the ire of Israel's elite. The religious authorities begin to plot Jesus's demise. They attempt to trap him with questions about fasting (5:33–39) and his activity on the Sabbath (6:1–11).

The next several chapters flesh out what Luke has already introduced. In the Sermon on the Plain (6:17–49), Jesus, as a new Moses, asserts that kingdom living is marked by radical love for God and one another. The faith of the centurion, a God-fearer, reminds the readers that the nations are joining Israel by faith alone (7:1–10). The parables of the soils and the mystery of the kingdom (8:4–18) explain why some accept Jesus's kingdom message and others reject it. Jesus anchors the theological basis of such large-scale rejection in the prophecy of Isaiah 6:9 (Luke 8:10). In light of the Isaiah 6 quotation, Jesus has come to judge those who cling to their idols of human tradition. Even Jesus's own family is having difficulty in understanding his identity and mission (Luke 8:19–21).

In the memorable stilling of the storm, Jesus explicitly identifies with Yahweh as he silences the raging sea (8:22–24). Only Israel's God possesses such power (see Pss. 89:9; 107:29; Isa. 51:9–10). The disciples, too, struggle with understanding Jesus in the stilling of the storm. Their question, "Who then is this?" (Luke 8:25), rings throughout the narrative. Jesus is more than Israel's King. He's

---

9   Craig L. Blomberg, after discussing purported parallels to the Greco-Roman symposium, rightly argues, "If we are to look for parallels to other banquets, we would do far better to see anticipations of the eschatological and Messianic banquet for which so many Jews longed" (*Contagious Holiness: Jesus' Meals with Sinners*, NSBT 19 [Leicester, UK: Apollos, 2005], 162).

Israel's Lord. After Jesus feeds the five thousand (9:10–17), the disciples have a breakthrough. Peter finally confesses that Jesus is "God's Messiah" (9:20 CSB). Herein lies the key to unlocking Jesus's identity: Jesus of Nazareth is both Yahweh incarnate and the anointed King of Israel. He is the Son of God and the Son of David. The angel Gabriel was right to predict, "He will be great and will be called *the Son of the Most High*. And the Lord God will give him the throne of *his father David*" (1:32). Jesus is truly fulfilling Old Testament expectations, but the way in which these predictions are being fulfilled is surprising.

Not permitting his disciples to get too comfortable with the title "God's Messiah," Jesus immediately qualifies it. He informs them that the "Son of Man must suffer many things . . . and be killed, and on the third day be raised" (9:22). This is the first of six passion predictions (9:44; 12:50; 13:32–33; 17:25; 18:31–33) that sets the tone for the remainder of Luke's narrative.[10]

Jesus's Journey to Jerusalem (9:51–19:27)

After the transfiguration, an event that demonstrates Jesus's status as cosmic Lord (9:28–36; see discussion in chapter 6), the time has come for Jesus to head south to Jerusalem to celebrate Passover. Though the three Synoptics record Jesus's journey from Galilee to Jerusalem, Luke reserves more than one-third of his narrative to the journey (see Matt. 19:1–20:34; Mark 8:22–10:52; Luke 9:51–19:27). Luke discloses that Jesus "set his face to go to Jerusalem" (9:51; cf. Isa. 50:7). To ascend to the Father's right hand, the climax of Jesus's ministry (Luke 24:50–52), Jesus must first endure the horrors of the cross in Jerusalem.

Along the journey, Jesus often speaks in parables to the crowds. Parables occupy a significant portion of the Third Gospel. There are about twenty-seven parables in Luke's Gospel, comprising about two-thirds of Jesus's total parables found in all the Gospels. Out of those

---

10   David E. Garland, *Luke*, ZECNT (Grand Rapids, MI: Zondervan, 2011), 245.

twenty-seven, approximately half are unique to this Gospel,[11] and the bulk of these parables are found on the road to Jerusalem. Why are they so prominent in this section? Jesus's teaching in 9:51–19:27 expands much of what he asserted in the Sermon on the Plain (6:17–49). The same principles of kingdom living are fleshed out, and Jesus engages his audience with parables that seize the reader's attention. The narrative slows almost to a snail's pace, forcing Luke's readers to consider the various layers of meaning each parable figuratively conveys. Luke 1:5–9:50 introduces the readers to the person and work of Jesus, whereas 9:51–19:27 expresses what following the Son of Man personally entails.

Jesus commissions seventy-two disciples (10:1–17), a group that signifies restored humanity and the reversal of the scattering of seventy-two people groups at Babel in Genesis 10-11.[12] These disciples continue to fulfill the prophecy of Genesis 3:15 in overthrowing the demons (Luke 10:19), prompting Jesus to declare that he "saw Satan fall like lightning from heaven" (10:18, partially quoting Isa. 14:12). The careers of the devil and Jesus are asymmetrical. Jesus becomes humble and low to be exalted to the Father's throne. The devil begins with a state of exaltation as the prince of the cosmos but, on account of Jesus's work, descends into a state of lowliness and subjugation.

The narrative progresses to the parable of the good Samaritan (Luke 10:25–37) and instruction concerning the Lord's prayer (11:1–13). The Beelzebul controversy reminds the readers that some of the crowd remain hostile to Jesus's ministry (11:14–26). The farther south Jesus travels, the more antagonistic the crowd becomes. Jesus issues a series of woes against the Pharisees for being more concerned with scruples of purity than with the integrity of the human heart (11:37–54). His teaching contained in the next several chapters leads to a crisis: the crowds must prize the kingdom above earthly authorities and material possessions. Jesus drives this point

---

11   Klyne R. Snodgrass, *Stories with Intent: A Comprehensive Guide to the Parables of Jesus* (Grand Rapids, MI: Eerdmans, 2008), 23.

12   See discussion of the seventy-two disciples in chapter 2.

home using a variety of parables (e.g., 14:25–35; 17:1–10; 18:1–8) and direct confrontations with the religious leaders (e.g., 13:31–35; 14:1–14; 15:1–32; 16:1–31; 18:9–30).

The sixth and final passion prediction (18:31–33) immediately precedes Jesus's arrival in Jericho, where he heals a blind beggar (18:35–43). In contrast to the religious authorities who reject Jesus, Luke supplies two examples of those on society's margins who place their faith in him. Though blind, this man spiritually perceives Jesus's identity as the "Son of David" (18:38–39). Another person, a chief tax collector named Zacchaeus, welcomes Jesus with open arms (19:1–10). Remarkably, Jesus declares that Zacchaeus is now a genuine "son of Abraham" (19:9). Whereas some Jewish leaders have attempted to earn that very status through works (see 18:9), Zacchaeus gains it on account of solely trusting in Jesus. As a result of following Jesus, he promises to repay those he's defrauded (19:8).

Jesus's Death and Resurrection in Jerusalem (19:28–24:53)

The third and final movement in Luke's Gospel takes place in Jerusalem where Jesus celebrates Passover. Luke (and the other three Evangelists) ramps up his use of the Old Testament during Jesus's final week of ministry, insisting that, at every point, the Old Testament anticipated it. It may seem that God's plan of redemption is spiraling out of control, but nothing could be further from the truth. In the triumphal entry, on Sunday of Passion Week, Jesus publicly announces his kingship (19:28–36). Those who witnessed Jesus riding on a donkey, a clear demonstration of his messiahship (see Zech. 9:9), and observed Jesus's preceding "mighty works" cry out, "Blessed is the King who comes in the name of the Lord! Peace in heaven and glory in the highest!" (Luke 19:37–38). These pilgrims cite Psalm 118:26, a Davidic psalm, and pin their hopes for political deliverance on Jesus.

Luke is the only Evangelist to include the Pharisees' opposition to Jesus immediately following the triumphal entry (Luke 19:39). The Pharisees represent the nation of Israel. Their antagonism toward him provokes Jesus to weep over the city of Jerusalem in 19:41–44. He explicitly ties the destruction of Jerusalem to Israel's rejection of him (19:43–44; 21:5–36). The narrative immediately progresses to Jesus meting out judgment on the temple (19:45–46). As he drives out the merchants, he cites two Old Testament passages in 19:46: Isaiah 56:7 ("My house shall be a house of prayer") and Jeremiah 7:11 ("You have made it a den of robbers"), one a text of restoration and the other a reference to judgment. The first passage, a prophecy about the temple becoming a rallying point for the nations (Isa. 56:3–8), takes on special significance in Luke's Gospel. A major component of the Third Gospel is, as we have learned, outsiders gaining entrance into the kingdom by identifying with Jesus. Here Jesus reaffirms the true intent of the temple: God dwelling with all of humanity, regardless of ethnicity and rank. This is precisely what Jesus has accomplished throughout his ministry.

The Jewish leaders' animosity toward Jesus intensifies during Passion Week. They proactively look for a way to make Jesus incriminate himself by asking him questions on taxation (Luke 20:20–26). The Sadducees even attempt to wield the Old Testament against him in a question about marriage (20:27–40). But, at every turn, Jesus remains firmly in the right. The controversies climax in 20:41–44, when Jesus turns the tables on the Jewish leaders by questioning their expectations of a coming Messiah. The Messiah cannot simply be a descendant of King David, because David himself confessed him as "Lord" (20:42–43, quoting Ps. 110:1). The Messiah must be simultaneously a son of David and Yahweh incarnate, precisely what Luke has demonstrated in his Gospel.

The narrative then progresses to the Olivet Discourse, where Jesus predicts the fall of Jerusalem in AD 70 (Luke 21:5–36). The disciples were taken aback at the beauty of the temple and how it was "adorned with noble stones and offerings" (21:5). But Jesus sees through the opulent veneer and perceives the temple for what it is: an outmoded, idolatrous building. God's glory is dwelling with his people in a more powerful and intimate way through Christ, so a physical building is no longer required (see Isa. 66:1; Jer. 3:16). The temple itself, too, has ironically become a bastion of pride and rebellion (19:46b). This two-fold problem explains why Jesus announces its destruction.

After Jesus predicts the nation's demise, the Jewish leaders broker a deal with Judas concerning Jesus's arrest (Luke 22:1–6). Jesus and the disciples celebrate the Passover Thursday night (22:13–38), a day early because Jesus and the disciples were Galileans. Galileans were permitted to celebrate Passover a day early because of the crowds.[13] Jesus's death takes center stage as he consciously identifies himself as the ultimate Passover sacrifice: "This is my body, which is given for you" (22:19). In contrast to some of the disciples who desire to take pride of place in the kingdom (22:24), Jesus is the ultimate servant (22:26–27), who will be "numbered with the transgressors" (22:37). Here he partially quotes Isaiah 53:12, the most explicit text in Luke's Gospel, indeed the entire Old Testament, that predicts a suffering Messiah. "For what is written about me," Jesus declares, "has its fulfillment" (Luke 22:37).

Soon thereafter, Judas betrays Jesus in Gethsemane (22:39–48), and the soldiers drag Jesus before the Sanhedrin early Friday morning (22:66–71). The purpose of this trial is to charge him with sedition and deliver him to Pilate so that he will put Jesus to death. After stating that the Jewish leaders cannot grasp his messianic identity (22:67–68), Jesus claims to be the "Son of Man . . . seated at the right hand of the power of God" (22:69). Two Old Testament texts are in mind: Daniel 7:13–14 and Psalm 110:1. Jesus claims that he is not simply Israel's Messiah but her divine, preexistent Lord. Convinced that Jesus has committed blasphemy, the Sanhedrin is ready to act.

The Jewish leaders then escort Jesus to the Praetorium, where they officially charge him with "misleading" the nation of Israel and sedition against Rome (Luke 23:2). Pilate remains unconvinced, and he confers with Herod Antipas, who has governed Galilee and Perea since 4 BC. Jesus's silence frustrates Herod, but Herod has no choice but to return Jesus to Pilate (23:8–12). Pilate seeks to appease the Jewish authorities by beating Jesus and releasing him rather than Barabbas, a well-known

---

13 See the discussion in Eckhard J. Schnabel, *Jesus in Jerusalem: The Last Days* (Grand Rapids, MI: Eerdmans, 2018), 145–47.

seditionist and murderer (23:19). But the religious leaders would have none of it and demand that Pilate crucify Jesus (23:23).

Pilate crucifies Jesus on Friday between two criminals. One of the criminals asks Jesus to "remember" him (23:42). Then Jesus delivers one of the most memorable lines in the Third Gospel: "Truly, I say to you, today you will be with me in paradise" (23:43). The term "paradise" (*paradeisos*) often refers to the garden of Eden, where God dwelled intimately with Adam and Eve (e.g., LXX Gen. 2:8, 9, 10, 15, 16; Ezek. 28:13). Jesus, therefore, promises the criminal intimate fellowship in the eternal new cosmos (see 2 Cor. 12:3–4; Rev. 2:7). Such a promise must be understood in light of Jesus's larger prerogative of communing with outsiders in Luke's Gospel.

"On the first day of the week," two days after Jesus's death, a group of women travel to the tomb only to discover it empty (Luke 24:1–3). Two angels "in dazzling apparel" greet the women, announcing that "he [Jesus] is not here, but has risen" (24:4–6). The angels inform the women that Jesus's resurrection is in keeping with his own prediction that he will be crucified and then raised "on the third day" (24:7; see 9:22, 44; 18:32–33). The women are quick to remember these prophecies and then relate to the disciples and to "all the rest" what they have witnessed, but the disciples "did not believe them" (24:8–11). Not only did the disciples fail to believe Jesus's six passion predictions, but they also refuse to believe the women's report. Peter, though, travels to the empty tomb and returns home "marveling at what had happened" (24:12).

Jesus's second journey, from Jerusalem to Emmaus (24:13–35), repeats the first journey from Galilee to Jerusalem (9:51–19:27) but with a stark difference: the disciples now understand the totality of Jesus's ministry (see the discussion in chapter 4). In the first journey, the disciples struggled to comprehend the nature of the various aspects of Jesus's ministry, particularly his death and resurrection. This explains why the journey is studded with parables. But on the road to Emmaus, Jesus graciously opens the minds of his disciples, giving them eyes to see and ears to hear. While Jesus applies Isaiah 6:9 to the "others" (i.e., the crowd) in Luke 8:10, there's still a sense in which the disciples remain partially blind and ignorant of Jesus's identity. To state the matter succinctly, the road to Emmaus tangibly demonstrates how Jesus's life, death, and resurrection fulfill the entire sweep of redemptive history. This is precisely what Luke promised to achieve at the beginning of his Gospel (1:1–4).

Two disciples, Cleopas and another unnamed, encounter Jesus on the road to Emmaus. They don't recognize Jesus, however, and proceed to catch him up to speed with what has transpired in Jerusalem the last few days. The two disciples relate how Jesus "was a prophet" whom the "chief priests and rulers delivered . . . up to be condemned to death" (24:19–20). Then the two narrate the discovery of the empty tomb by the women and Peter, but they remain unconvinced (24:22–24). Jesus responds with a scathing indictment of the two:

> "O foolish ones, and slow of heart to believe *all that the prophets have spoken*! Was it not necessary that the Christ should suffer these things and enter into his glory?" And beginning with *Moses and all the Prophets*, he interpreted to them *in all the Scriptures* the things concerning himself. (24:25–27)

Later in the day when Jesus miraculously appears to his disciples, he pursues the same line of thinking:

> "These are my words that I spoke to you while I was still with you, that everything written about me *in the Law of Moses and the Prophets and the Psalms* must be fulfilled." Then he opened their minds to understand the Scriptures, and said to them, "Thus it is written, that the Christ should suffer and on the third day rise from the dead, and that repentance for the forgiveness of sins should be proclaimed in his name to all nations, beginning from Jerusalem." (24:44–47)

Scholars vigorously debate how Christ relates to the Old Testament, but wading into these deep waters is beyond the scope of this project.

However, in light of these two passages, four critical yet brief thoughts are in order.

First, the totality of the Old Testament anticipates Christ's death and resurrection. Most scholars argue that only a handful of Old Testament texts *explicitly* anticipate a coming Messiah figure (e.g., Isa. 11; Jer. 23:5; Ezek. 34:23; Zech. 9:9), and even fewer argue that the Old Testament expects a suffering Messiah. But this is not how Jesus (and the apostles) reads the Old Testament. He claims that the whole of the Old Testament anticipates his life, death, and resurrection (see John 5:39–47; 1 Cor. 15:3–4; 1 Pet. 1:10–11).

Second, by tracking Luke's use of Old Testament quotations and allusions and tracing how he relates Old Testament themes, we can get a concrete sense of how Jesus fulfills the totality of Israel's Scriptures.[14] Luke keeps his readers' attention attuned to the Old Testament throughout his Gospel. While we were unable to note every instance where Luke invoked the Old Testament, we still gained some sense of how Luke generally relates the Old Testament to Jesus. To name a few, Luke presents Jesus as the long-awaited, virgin-born Son of King David (Luke 1:69; 2:4; 6:1–5), the last Adam and the true Israel of God (3:38–4:13), the Messiah announcing the eschatological year of jubilee (4:18–19), the rejected prophet of Israel (4:24–27), Yahweh incarnate who redeems his people in the second exodus and leads his people to the promised land of the new creation (3:4–6; 9:51–19:27; 20:42–43), the new Moses (6:12–49), Daniel's Son of Man (9:21–36; 21:27; 22:69), Isaiah's suffering servant (1:32; 22:37), the new temple (19:45–46), the resurrected one (24:1–12), and the great interpreter of Israel's Scriptures (24:25–27, 44–47).

Third, one salient reason why the disciples (and the majority of the Israelites) misunderstood Jesus lies in *how* Jesus fulfills the Old Testament. For example, the Old Testament contains a bundle of themes that appear to be unrelated on the surface: temple, second exodus,

---

14 Another avenue into Luke's use of the Old Testament as it relates to Christ is his use of Scripture in the book of Acts. For an excellent overview, see Alan J. Thompson, "Acts, Book of," in *Dictionary of the New Testament Use of the Old Testament*.

coming Messiah, kingdom, covenant curses and blessings, end-time suffering and tribulation, descent of the Spirit, forgiveness of sin, justification, restoration of true Israel, and so on. Yes, the Old Testament expected that these themes and events would come to fruition at the end of history in "the days to come" / "the latter days" (see Gen. 49:1; Num. 24:14; Deut. 4:30; 31:29; Hos. 3:5; Isa. 2:2; Ezek. 38:14–16; Dan. 2:28–29, 45). But the Old Testament does not explicitly bring them together *in the coming Messiah*. In other words, Jesus mysteriously pulls together seemingly disparate redemptive-historical threads and consciously fulfills them *in himself*.[15] Like spokes protruding from a wheel, Jesus, the center of redemptive history, fuses these themes together in his ministry. Take, for example, Jesus's identity as Adam / true Israel in the wilderness temptation. Whereas the first generation of Israelites was unfaithful in the wilderness and succumbed to idolatry, Jesus as Adam / true Israel faithfully trusted in God's promises (Luke 3:38–4:13). A handful of chapters later, Jesus, as Yahweh incarnate, stills the storm (8:22–25). Jesus is Israel and Yahweh! Though the Old Testament may hint at a divine Messiah (see Ps. 110:1; Isa. 9:6; Dan. 7:13–14; Mic. 5:2), it was largely unexpected that the coming Messiah would be both Israel's (suffering!) King and her divine Lord. These two redemptive-historical spokes come together in the person of Christ.

Fourth, not only does Jesus wed various Old Testament themes, he also typologically fulfills prominent Old Testament events, institutions, and persons. Every verse, paragraph, and chapter, in some way, prophetically anticipates the person of Christ. Most Christians today believe that Jesus only fulfills explicit verbal prophecies in the Old Testament, such as Isaiah 11:1–16 and Zechariah 9:9, but that is only

---

15 The biblical category of "mystery" is helpful, particularly as it relates to how New Testament authors read the Old Testament in light of Christ. Complete or full meaning of large swaths of the Old Testament was partially "hidden" but now has been fully "revealed" in Christ. A Christological reading of the Old Testament was really present in the text, but it was latent or hidden. Now that Christ has come, the full meaning of the Old Testament is revealed (see discussion in G. K. Beale and Benjamin L. Gladd, *Hidden but Now Revealed: A Biblical Theology of Mystery* [Downers Grove, IL: IVP Academic, 2014], 291–93, 328–38).

one dimension of how Jesus relates to the Old Testament. Yes, he fulfills verbal prophecies, but he also fulfills Old Testament patterns, types, and institutions. R. T. France, though he's commenting on the nature of fulfillment in Matthew's Gospel, is right to conclude,

> "Fulfillment" for Matthew seems to operate at many levels, embracing much more of the pattern of OT history and language than merely its prophetic predictions. It is a matter of tracing lines of correspondence and continuity in God's dealings with his people, discerned in the incidental details of the biblical text as well as in its grand design.[16]

The disciples were not reading the Old Testament rightly. They were failing to read Israel's Scriptures on "many levels" and failing to trace "lines of correspondence" between Israel's stories and Jesus.

Luke climactically ends his narrative with Jesus's departure into heaven (24:50–53; cf. Acts 1:9). The Third Gospel begins with Jesus's humble birth in a feeding trough (2:7) and ends with his exaltation to the Father's throne. His exaltation is critical to the story. Jesus sits enthroned not in a subordinate role; he doesn't rule over the nations from an earthly, physical throne in Jerusalem. Instead, as Richard Bauckham argues, "Jesus was exalted to sit with God on this very throne of the cosmos. This makes Jesus sovereign over 'all things.'"[17] His assumption to heaven demonstrates his incomparable rule over the universe, explaining why Luke has carefully woven Jesus's identity as Daniel's "Son of Man" and Israel's "Lord" into his narrative. Now that Jesus sits enthroned, he will pour out his Spirit on the church and empower his people to take the gospel to the "end of the earth" (Acts 1:8).

Conclusion

Luke penned his Gospel to convince Theophilus and Gentiles that Jesus is indeed the one whom the apostles proclaim and the one who

---

16 R. T. France, *The Gospel of Matthew*, NICNT (Grand Rapids, MI: Eerdmans, 2007), 13.

17 Richard Bauckham, "Is 'High Human Christology' Sufficient? A Critical Response to J. R. Daniel Kirk's *A Man Attested by God*," *BBR* 27:4 (2017): 508.

fulfills the whole of the Old Testament. Two titles largely strike at the heart of Luke's presentation of Jesus's identity: the Son of God and the Son of David. As the Son of God, Jesus is identified with Israel's God who redeems Israel from spiritual captivity in a second exodus. As the Son of David, Jesus inaugurates the long-awaited kingdom of God. Jesus not only faithfully adheres to the covenant, as a second Adam / true Israel figure, he also bears God's curse on behalf of the covenant community. Both forms of obedience, active and passive, establish the basis for the believer's justification.

Luke is thoroughly acquainted with the Old Testament. For Luke and the other Evangelists, the person of Jesus cannot be understood apart from Israel's Scriptures. Jesus doesn't simply fulfill one layer or stream of the Old Testament. He fulfills the whole of it. Related to the debate concerning the hermeneutical integrity of the apostles' use of the Old Testament is the question whether or not the church should follow suit. Should believers read and interpret the Old Testament like the apostles? Though many and perhaps the majority of commentators would answer in the negative, my contention is that the church today should interpret the Old Testament in accordance with the apostolic use of the Old Testament. The apostles learned to interpret and read the Old Testament through the Old Testament itself (the Old Testament prophets' use of antecedent revelation), the synagogue, family, and Jesus himself. Out of those four areas of instruction, Jesus is the primary resource. During his career and especially after his resurrection, he explained to the disciples how his ministry accords with the Old Testament and how Israel's Scriptures ultimately point to him. The question is, in reality, whether believers should interpret the Old Testament like Jesus. Since Jesus is the perfect Adam and Yahweh incarnate, his reading of the Old Testament is always valid and exemplary. If we should live like Jesus, we should also read like Jesus.

1

The Great Reversal

THE THIRD GOSPEL EMPLOYS the general term "high" or "highest" (*hypsos* and other similar terms) far more than any Gospel or book of the New Testament. It's not even close. Luke often describes God as the "most High" (1:32, 35, 76; 6:35; 8:28) and refers to heaven as the "highest" or "on high" (1:78; 2:14; 19:38; 24:49). On the other hand, downward movement is also pronounced. Mary states that God has "*brought down* [*katheilen*] the mighty" (1:52). Jesus asserts that Capernaum will be "*brought down* [*katabēsē*] to Hades" (10:15), and a few verses later he states, "I saw Satan *fall* [*pesonta*] like lightning from heaven" (10:18). Why such a vertical concern?

The answer lies in Mary's praise in the well-known Magnificat (1:46–55). Embedded within this song, Luke's vertical emphasis surfaces:

He [God] *has brought down the* mighty from their thrones
and *exalted* those of humble estate. (1:52)

This chapter attempts to carve out Luke's concern for the exaltation of the humble and the humiliation of the proud. Christ's humiliation in his life and especially in the cross qualifies him to be exalted to the Father's right hand.

Prophecies of Humiliation and Exaltation

The first two chapters of the Third Gospel establish the central themes of the book. Raymond Brown expresses this outlook when he states,

"In the first two chapters of the Gospel [of Luke] there is a transition from the story of Israel to the story of Jesus. There appear, almost from the pages of the Old Testament, characters like Zechariah and Elizabeth, Simeon and Anna, who are the final representatives of the piety of Israel."[1] The births of John and Jesus, then, flow from the larger story of Israel.

Luke's Gospel uniquely contains four hymns: 1:46–55 (the Magnificat), 1:68–79 (the Benedictus), 2:14 (Gloria in Excelsis), and 2:29–32 (the Nunc Dimittis). Each is named after the first few words in the Latin translation. These hymns, like those found elsewhere in Scripture, generally summarize the message of the Third Gospel (see, e.g., Dan. 2:20–23; 4:1–3, 34–35; 6:25–27). The first and the fourth hymns cry out for reflection.

The Magnificat

Much could be said about the Magnificat, but we will focus on two interrelated themes: (1) the overthrow of the mighty and the exaltation of the humble; (2) fulfillment of messianic expectations. A cursory read through the hymn reminds the reader of Hannah's prayer of thanksgiving for the birth of her son, Samuel (1 Sam. 2:1–10). The similarities between Hannah and Mary are striking, perhaps warranting a case of typology (see table 1.1).

Table 1.1   Comparison of Hannah and Mary

Hannah	Mary
Identifies herself as the Lord's "servant" (1 Sam. 1:11)	Identifies herself as the Lord's "servant" (Luke 1:38, 48)
Miraculous birth because of infertility (1 Sam. 1:5)	Virgin birth (Luke 1:34–35)
Extols God for the birth of Samuel (1 Sam. 2:1–10)	Extols God for the future birth of Jesus (Luke 1:46–55)
Hannah names her son Samuel (1 Sam. 1:20)	Angel instructs Mary to name her son Jesus (Luke 1:31)
Acknowledges that God exalts the poor and humble (1 Sam. 2:6–8)	Acknowledges that God brings down the proud but exalts the humble (Luke 1:52)

---

1   *The Birth of the Messiah: A Commentary on the Infancy Narratives in Matthew and Luke* (Garden City, NY: Image, 1977), 242.

Darrell Bock argues, "The strongest literary parallel to the hymn is Hannah's word of praise in 1 Sam. 2:1–10."[2] *If* Luke intends Mary's prayer to be modeled after Hannah's, then perhaps we should push a bit deeper into the immediate context of Hannah's prayer in 1 Samuel 2. Hannah confesses,

> There is none holy like the LORD:
>> for there is none besides you;
>> there is no rock like our God. (1 Sam. 2:2)

Then, *based on his utter uniqueness*, the Lord reverses present realities. He alone possesses the right and authority to bring down "mighty" warriors in judgment, and he "exalts" the weak to a lofty position of authority (1 Sam. 2:4, 7–8). In addition to a great reversal, we can also discern royal overtones woven throughout Hannah's prayer. According to 1 Samuel 2:8, God takes the "poor from the dust" and makes them "sit with princes and inherit a seat of honor." The word here for "seat" is probably better rendered as "throne" (see LXX, CSB, NIV), suggesting that the poor will inherit a prominent place of rule in the kingdom of God, perhaps at the end of history (cf. Ps. 113:7–8; Dan. 4:17). The final verse in the prayer zeroes in on the Lord's judgment falling on Israel's enemies through a royal figure:

> The LORD will judge the ends of the earth;
>> he will give strength to his king
>> and exalt the horn of his anointed. (1 Sam. 2:10; cf. Ps. 2:9)

While the readers aren't yet privy to the precise identification of this successful "king," they will soon discover that, at least initially, the referent is none other than King David.

As we compare and contrast Hannah's and Mary's prayers, several points of contact are worthy of consideration. But before we

---

2   Darrell L. Bock, *Luke 1:1–9:50*, BECNT (Grand Rapids, MI: Baker Academic, 1994), 148.

contemplate the two, let's take a moment to consider the incredible exchange between Mary and Elizabeth immediately before the Magnificat. According to Luke 1:41–43, Elizabeth, "filled with the Holy Spirit," acknowledges that Jesus is her "Lord" (*kyriou*). Luke has employed the term "Lord" (*kyrios*) ten times up to this point in the narrative, and each occurrence unambiguously refers to Israel's God (e.g., Luke 1:6, 9, 11, 16, 32). So, when Elizabeth confesses that the unborn Jesus is her "Lord," Luke has thoughtfully and carefully identified Jesus as Israel's Lord incarnate. Luke applies the term "Lord" to Jesus *and* to Israel's God, inviting the reader to bring both figures together. Further, Mary's declaration that she's a "servant of the Lord" (Luke 1:38), then, means that she is none other than a servant of her unborn baby.

This baby is the eternal Lord and the God of Israel. This is the same Lord whom Hannah extols in her prayer. If we reread 1 Samuel 2:2 in light of Luke 1, the result is incredible:

> There is none holy like the Lord [Jesus];
> for there is none beside you;
> there is no rock like our God. (1 Sam. 2:2)

Luke has placed Jesus squarely in an explicit, Israelite monotheistic confession. Further, and in this vein, Luke's readers should also assume that Israel's Lord who breaks the "bows of the mighty," "exalts" the "poor," and places his people among the "princes" (1 Sam. 2:4, 7–8) is none other than the preexistent Jesus—the second person of the Trinity. This identification doesn't exclude the other two persons of the Trinity, but it does include Jesus in Hannah's prayer. The mystery of the incarnation comes to the foreground in the Magnificat. How can the Lord, the God of Israel, the one who miraculously superintended the birth of Samuel and the virgin birth, be the same God as the unborn Jesus? As difficult as it is to wrap our heads around both of these truths, we must affirm both. Jesus is God *and* man. In the incarnation, the preexistent one added humanity to his deity. This may explain why Luke mentions that Elizabeth is "filled with the Holy Spirit" when she identifies Jesus as "Lord." Such incredible insight can only come from above.

According to Luke 1:51–53, Mary reaffirms Hannah's prayer of the great reversal of fortunes:[3]

> He has shown strength with his arm;
>   he has *scattered the proud* in the thoughts of their hearts;
> he *has brought down the* mighty from their thrones
>   and exalted those of humble estate;
> he has *filled the hungry* with good things,
>   and the rich he has sent away empty.

Luke puts his finger on the defeat of powers and the exaltation of the poor—an emphasis that runs throughout all of Luke-Acts. The Evangelist also explains *how* the Lord will do so: just as God redeemed Israel from the clutches of Egyptian slavery, he will deliver Israel once more and with great finality. The combination of words and expressions in the hymn, such as "the Mighty One" (1:49 CSB), "great things" (1:49), "holy is his name" (1:49), "strength" (1:51), "arm" (1:51), "scattered" (1:51), "thrones" (1:52), and "his servant Israel" (1:54), brings to mind the first exodus.[4] But, unlike the first exodus, God promises Mary that he will not redeem Israel primarily from political might but from the

---

3   One interpretative difficulty is wrestling with the six aorist verbs in 1:51–53. Several options exist. For example, do the aorist verbs refer to past events? Or do they refer to what will transpire in the future? Bock rightly argues that they are "prophetic aorists," verbs that are "portraying the ultimate eschatological events tied to Jesus' final victory" (Bock, *Luke 1:1–9:50*, 155). I contend, though, that these prophetic aorists are initially fulfilled throughout the totality of Christ's ministry, particularly in the wilderness temptation and not simply in his death and resurrection (see discussion below).

4   See the discussion in David W. Pao and Eckhard J. Schnabel, "Luke," in *Commentary on the New Testament Use of the Old Testament*, ed. G. K. Beale and D. A. Carson (Grand Rapids, MI: Baker Academic, 2007), 261–62. François Bovon even connects the Magnificat to Exodus 15: "The model of all songs of praise in Israel remains the hymn recounting the miraculous parting of the Red Sea" (*Luke 1: A Commentary on the Gospel of Luke 1:1–9:50*, Hermeneia, trans. Christine M. Thomas [Minneapolis: Fortress, 2002], 57).

powers of sin and the devil.[5] Consummate redemption will occur only at the second coming of Christ, not at his first coming.

We would also do well to contemplate the larger context of Hannah's prayer and the overall thrust of 1–2 Samuel. The prophet Samuel played no small role in the establishment of the Davidic dynasty (e.g., 1 Sam. 16:1–13). But while David was certainly remarkable on several levels, internal strife and personal sins dogged his reign. King David was not Israel's solution to defeating God's enemies and overcoming wickedness—that is reserved for one of his descendants (2 Sam. 7). A faithful, pristine Adam figure remained a future reality. In the end, Hannah's prayer goes beyond David (and Solomon), finding its ultimate fulfillment in Jesus, *the* Son of David (see Luke 1:32–33). In sum, *God will bring down all forms of rule, physical and spiritual, through King Jesus and redeem his people in the second exodus.*

The Nunc Dimittis

When Jesus is born, Joseph and Mary take him to the temple for dedication (2:22; see discussion in chapter 3). At the temple, they cross paths with a man named Simeon, an individual "waiting for the consolation of Israel" (2:25). After he blesses baby Jesus, he turns to Mary and predicts, "Behold, this child is appointed for *the fall* and *rising* of many in Israel" (2:34). The blessing is admirably close to Mary's expectation in 1:52 that the Lord "has brought down" rulers and "exalted" the feeble in the birth of Jesus. Simeon's cryptic line reinforces Mary's prediction that Jesus will generate the great reversal of fortunes. Herein lies the brilliance of Simeon's words: God's victory over all forms of authorities paves the way for the marginalized and the Gentiles to participate in the covenant community, thereby fulfilling the prophecy of Isaiah 49:6:

> It is too light a thing that you should be my servant
>   to raise up the tribes of Jacob

---

5   Raymond Brown suggests, "The poverty and hunger of the oppressed in the Magnificat are primarily spiritual" (*The Birth of the Messiah*, 363).

and to bring back the preserved of Israel;
  I will make you as a light for the nations,
    that my salvation may reach to the end of the earth.

The toppling of earthly and heavenly powers is directly tied to the influx of the destitute and the nations. The vertical and the horizontal are fused together. This observation explains why Luke often mentions the toppling of Satan's power and influence mediated through his demons (e.g., Luke 4:1–13, 33–36, 41; 8:2, 27–33; 9:1; 10:17; 13:32). In vanquishing the demonic powers, Jesus unshackles those whom the devil has long held captive—the marginalized and the Gentiles (see discussion in chapter 2).

Defeat of Spiritual and Physical Powers

The remaining portion of the chapter will trace the great reversal in the remainder of Luke's Gospel. I will first isolate a few instances of Christ's victory over political and spiritual powers and then consider a smattering of texts that underscore the exaltation of the lowly.

The Defeat of the Devil and the Demons

I will devote an entire section to the wilderness temptation in chapter 6, so I need only mention a few important details. The wilderness temptation contains a great deal of significance for Jesus's earthly ministry. Here Jesus initially defeats the devil and begins to overthrow his kingdom. Here also Jesus begins to establish God's eternal, end-time kingdom. For my purposes, I will focus only on one dimension.

In the second temptation, Luke's account graphically narrates the devil taking Jesus "up" (Luke 4:5), but only Matthew discloses where the devil takes him—"to a very high mountain" (Matt. 4:8). Then, in the third and climactic temptation, the devil takes Jesus to the "pinnacle of the temple," where the devil entices Jesus to "throw [himself] down from here," promising him angelic intervention by citing Psalm 91:11–12 (Luke 4:9–11). The second half of the quotation reads, "They [the angels] will bear you *up*" (4:11). Luke's spatial language of "up" and "down" is hard to miss, but commentators often neglect the symbolism behind the language. Perhaps Luke wants his audience to view the wilderness temptation through the lens of 1:52 and 2:34. If so, the devil, attempting to mirror Yahweh's prerogative to exalt and bring down, intends to do the same to Jesus. He brings Jesus up, and then commands him to go down—only to assure him, in the third temptation, of being once more lifted up. *The devil wants Jesus to join him in his exalted or "lifted up" state of rule by breaking God's commandments.* In the end, the third temptation shortcuts the humiliation of the cross.[6]

Jesus would have none of it. Instead of obeying the devil, Jesus obeys his Father. The results are twofold: (1) Jesus's faithfulness in the wilderness temptation initially casts the devil down from his heavenly position (see discussion below), so that (2) Jesus could be exalted and assume a cosmic rule. Jesus and the devil switch locations as it were. As a result of Adam's fall, God sovereignly and temporarily ordains the devil with the right to rule over the cosmos (see e.g., Job 1:6–12; 2:7). The apostle John says, after all, that Satan is the "ruler of this world" (John 12:31; cf. Rev. 12:7–12). Christ's victory in the wilderness initially but decisively dislodges the devil's rule over the cosmos. The cross and resurrection then deepen Christ's reign (John 12:31; Col. 2:15; Heb. 2:14). At the second coming, Christ will consummately defeat Satan and bring him down to the lake of fire (Rev. 20:10).

Immediately following the wilderness temptation, Jesus ministers in Galilee and arrives in his hometown of Nazareth, where he is famously rejected after proclaiming the fulfillment of Isaiah 61:1–2 (Luke 4:16–30). The Nazarenes attempt to "throw him down the cliff" (4:29). A careful reader of Luke's Gospel will immediately see the connection with the third temptation. In attempting to throw Jesus down, they are symbolically attempting to dethrone Jesus. But the Nazarenes are unsuccessful as Jesus walked right "through their midst" (4:30).

---

6   Joel B. Green comes close to this line of reasoning when he maintains, "The devil has an alternative aim, a competing agenda. He wants to recruit Jesus to participate in a test of the divine promises of Psalm 91. . . . The devil fails to recognize . . . that divine rescue may come *through* suffering and death and not only *before* (and *from*) them" (*The Gospel of Luke*, NICNT [Grand Rapids, MI: Eerdmans, 1997], 198 [italics original]).

Jesus begins exorcising demons, demonstrating that he is indeed the ruler of the cosmos (see 4:31–37, 41; 8:26–39). Then, in Luke 9, we discern a subtle yet important shift. Jesus empowers his followers to participate in the overthrow of Satan's domain. They reap the benefits of his obedience. According to 9:1, Jesus "gave [the twelve] power and authority over all demons." The wording here is built on the prophecy of Daniel 7:14 and 7:27 (see discussion in chapter 6) and remarkably close to the devil promising to "give . . . authority" to Jesus in the wilderness temptation (Luke 4:6). Jesus's behavior follows precisely the pattern laid out in Daniel 7, where the Ancient of Days first gives authority to rule over the kingdom to the Son of Man (Dan. 7:13–14) and then gives authority to rule over the kingdom to the "saints of the Most High" (Dan. 7:27). As the successful Son of Man who inherited the authority to rule over the cosmos, Jesus appoints twelve disciples to rule with him and enjoy authority over the demons. Later in Luke 10, Jesus appoints an additional seventy-two disciples, probably representing renewed humanity (see Gen. 10–11), to proclaim the presence of the kingdom (Luke 10:1–11). When the seventy-two disciples return from their mission, they exclaim, "Lord, even the demons are subject to us in your name" (Luke 10:17). Jesus responds with one of the most cryptic lines in the Third Gospel: "I saw Satan fall like lightning from heaven" (Luke 10:18).

The various options for interpreting this verse are as many as the commentators themselves. We need not get bogged down in some of the finer points of this passage. Our goal here is to view the verse through the lens of 1:52 and 2:34. In 10:18 Luke's readers are again struck with the spatial dimension: "I saw Satan fall . . . from heaven." Jesus's emphasis on the downward movement fits quite well with our contention that 1:52 and 2:34 are programmatic to Luke's Gospel. The great reversal of fortunes has occurred. Luke 10:18 also alludes to Isaiah 14:12:

How you are fallen from heaven,
    O Day Star, son of Dawn!
How you are cut down to the ground,
    you who laid the nations low!

Jesus has in mind not merely a single verse but the entire thrust of Isaiah 13–14. In the immediate context, Israel has endured great hardship in exile and has subsequently returned to the promised land (Isa. 14:1–2), where they taunt the "king of Babylon" for his pride and wickedness in enslaving the nation (Isa. 14:4). The king(s) will be "laid low" to Sheol (i.e., "the realm of the dead," NIV) which welcomes the king with open arms (Isa.14:8–11). The next several verses explain why he will be cast down. In Isaiah 14:13–14, the audience learns the motivation of the king's heart:

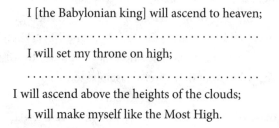

> I [the Babylonian king] will ascend to heaven;
> . . . .
> I will set my throne on high;
> . . . .
> I will ascend above the heights of the clouds;
> I will make myself like the Most High.

His attempt to rule alongside God is met by divine opposition, and God casts him down to the earth. But notice that the king falls *below* earth—into the underworld or Sheol (Isa. 14:9, 15).

Luke's use of Isaiah 14 is quite sophisticated, more than what scholars often recognize. Jesus clearly identifies Satan with the king of Babylon. But why? Perhaps for a couple of reasons: (1) The Israelites taunt the Babylonian king because the oppressor of Israel has become the oppressed. Their roles have been reversed. In the Gospels, the true tyrant is not Rome but Satan, the individual standing behind all forms of oppressive leadership. He has enslaved humanity from the fall of Adam and Eve onward. But Christ's victory in the wilderness broke the devil's hold on humanity, releasing God's people from spiritual exile. (2) The downfall of the king of Babylon or the "Day Star" signals the fulfillment of Isaiah's second exodus. According to Isaiah 13:10–13,

> The *stars* of the heavens and their constellations
>   will not give their light;

the sun will be dark at its rising,
> and the moon will not shed its light.

. . . .

I will make the heavens tremble,
> and the earth will be shaken out of its place.

Such cosmic-conflagration language evokes the tectonic shift of empires. True to apocalypticism, the heavens mirror the events on earth. When one earthly kingdom eclipses another, the cosmic conflagration inevitably results.[7] So when Jesus sees Satan, the "Day Star," falling from heaven, he's reassuring his disciples that the second exodus is well underway, and they should remain confident that their efforts are playing a critical role in dismantling the kingdom of Satan. God's eternal kingdom is eclipsing Satan's temporary kingdom. One kingdom falls and another rises. Jesus's victory in the wilderness fuels the success of his disciples (note Jesus's allusion to Gen. 3:15 and Ps. 91:13 in Luke 10:19).

The Defeat of Political and Religious Authorities

Luke applies imagery of rising and falling not only to invisible realities but also to other important dimensions. I will now examine a few examples that bespeak the rise and fall of political and religious parties. One unique feature of Luke's Gospel is his penchant for relating Jesus's life to the larger Roman world. At the beginning of Luke 2, he states, "In those days a decree went out from Caesar Augustus that all the world should be registered. This was the first registration when Quirinius was governor of Syria" (2:1–2). Then, in Luke 3, he historically contextualizes John's and Jesus's public ministries: "In the fifteenth year of the reign of Tiberius Caesar, Pontius Pilate being governor of Judea, and Herod being tetrarch of Galilee, and his brother Philip tetrarch of the region of Ituraea and Trachonitis, and Lysanias tetrarch of Abilene, during

---

7 See, e.g., Isa. 24:1–6, 19–23; 34:4; Jer. 4:23–28; Ezek. 32:6–8; Dan. 8:10; Matt. 24:29; Mark 13:24; Luke 21:25–28; Rom. 16:20; Rev. 9:1; 12:9.

the high priesthood of Annas and Caiaphas" (3:1–2). Why mention all these political rulers? Perhaps Luke partly roots his account in the larger context of the world political system because he's convinced of their eventual demise and the eternality of Christ's rule.

What if Mary's prediction that God would bring "down the mighty from their thrones" (1:52) included not only Satan and his minions but also these political rulers? Caesar Augustus and Tiberius Caesar, while certainly lofty figures in their day, eventually turned to dust. The Roman Empire, too, a mighty war machine, eventually collapsed. But the kingdom that Jesus inaugurated, while seemingly small and insignificant at its beginning, has grown into a towering oak (see 13:18–19). Who would have thought that Jesus, born in the humblest of circumstances and under one of the mightiest political figures in history, Caesar Augustus, would eventually ascend to the Father's throne to rule over the far reaches of the cosmos? At the end of the book of Acts, we discover the apostle Paul under house arrest in Rome where he was boldly "proclaiming the kingdom of God and teaching about the *Lord* Jesus Christ" (Acts 28:31). The gospel has come to the seat of the Roman Empire. The true King or "Lord" sits not on an earthly throne but on the very throne of heaven.

In addition to the fall of political rulers, Luke includes the religious sphere. We stumble on a clue in Simeon's speech early in the narrative: "Behold, this child [Jesus] is appointed for *the fall and rising of many in Israel*" (Luke 2:34). Those who enjoy positions of honor "in Israel" will be humiliated, whereas those of little or no influence will be elevated. The question remains, though: who identifies with the positions of honor, and who identifies with the position of the lowly in the Third Gospel? My concern here is to answer the first part of the question, and then I will turn to the second part at the end of the chapter.

The first form of resistance to Jesus's ministry arrives in 5:17–26 when Jesus announces the forgiveness of a paralytic's sins before healing him (5:20). The Pharisees and the "teachers of the law" (5:17) quickly object because no one can forgive sins "but God alone" (5:21). As the narrative moves forward, the interaction between Jesus and the Jewish leaders intensifies and their hostility increases (see, e.g., 6:7–11; 7:30; 11:37–54). One terrific example arrives in 14:1–14, where Jesus, after healing a man and silencing the Pharisees (14:1–6), furnishes two parables to his audience that recall 1:52 and 2:34. The first parable entails a wedding celebration where the guests should pursue the "lowest place" and not the "place of honor" (14:8–10; see Prov 25:6–7). Then, in 14:11, Jesus explains why: "For everyone *who exalts* [*ho hypsōn*] himself *will be humbled* [*tapeinōthēsetai*], and *he who humbles* [*ho tapeinōn*] himself *will be exalted* [*hypsōthēsetai*]" (cf. James 4:10).[8] The wording evokes what we find earlier in the programmatic Luke 1:52: "he has brought down the mighty from their thrones and *exalted those of humble estate* [*hypsōsen tapeinous*]." Luke 14:11 once more affirms a salient characteristic of Luke's Gospel, but in this case, the wording is explicitly tethered to the Jewish leaders. If they do not bow the knee to the Son of Man in great humility, then God promises to cut them down with a sword of judgment.

Exaltation of the Humble

In the final portion of this chapter, I turn my attention to the exaltation of the lowly. Luke's concern for the poor and marginalized is apparent, as commentators often point out, but it often goes unnoticed that Luke's portrayal of the marginalized flows from 1:52 and 2:34. I will first trace this theme in Jesus's followers and then Jesus himself, who humbles himself on the cross and subsequently ascends to the Father's right hand.

Exaltation of the Marginalized

While the four Gospels emphasize the marginalized in society, Luke's Gospel especially highlights this theme. There are too many instances to canvas, so I will confine my discussion to two examples that depict the exaltation of the lowly.

---

8   See also Sir. 3:19 and Let. Aris. 263.

The first example is well known and unique to the Third Gospel. The parable of the rich man and Lazarus (16:19–31), one of the most riveting and graphic parables in Luke's narrative, explains the eternal outcome of a life devoted to wealth and pleasure.[9] The parable of the unjust steward (16:1–8) encourages Luke's audience to use their wealth wisely, whereas this parable explains what will befall those who refuse. While characters in parables often go unnamed, the poor man in this parable is called Lazarus. What's the significance? *Lazarus* is the Greek name for the Hebrew *Eliezer*, a name that means "God helps" (see Ex. 18:4). "God helps" the poor man in contrast to the rich man who helps himself. Luke clearly juxtaposes the rich man with Lazarus, before and after death (see table 1.2).

Table 1.2   Comparison of the Rich Man and Lazarus

The Rich Man before Death	Lazarus before Death
"clothed in purple and fine linen" (16:19)	"covered with sores" (16:20)
"feasted sumptuously" (16:19)	begged for food (16:21)
"received . . . good things" (16:25)	received "bad things" (16:25)

The Rich Man after Death	Lazarus after Death
endures an unquenchable fire (16:24)	dines with Abraham (16:23)
lives "in torment" and "anguish" (16:23, 25)	lives in comfort (16:25)

Death is the turning point for both individuals. God has exalted the lowly Lazarus and cast down the exalted rich man. The parable also subtly displays a vertical concern, falling very much in line with our thesis. God assigns the rich man to Hades, whereas he places Lazarus at Abraham's "side" (16:23). The term *Hades* here means "underworld" or "the realm of the dead." Abraham's "side" and Hades are two antithetical locations—one up and one down. According to

9   The discussion of Luke 16:19–31 has been excerpted and adapted from pages 270–71 of *Handbook on the Gospels* by Benjamin L. Gladd, copyright © 2021. Used by permission of Baker Academic, a division of Baker Publishing Group.

16:23, the rich man "*lifted up* [*eparas*] his eyes," reinforcing Luke's vertical concern. Earlier in 10:15, we find something quite similar: "And you, Capernaum, will you be exalted to *heaven*? You shall be brought down to *Hades.*" Heaven and hades are polar opposites. Furthermore, between the upper and lower realms is a "great chasm" that had "been fixed" (16:26), not permitting either party to join the other (cf. 1 En. 18.11–12; 22:8–13). Lazarus was barred from the rich man's palace by a gate in his earthly life (Luke 16:20), but the rich man is now barred from heaven.[10] The upper and lower realms cannot be traversed. What this means, then, is that those exalted on earth only enjoy their place of honor for a short time, but the lowly will be exalted for all of eternity.

The second example may seem odd at first but makes beautiful sense in light of our discussion. Toward the end of his journey to Jerusalem, Jesus ventures through Jericho, where Zacchaeus, a "chief tax collector," desires to see him (19:1–3). Tax collectors occupy no small role in Luke's narrative and often follow Jesus with eagerness (see 3:12; 5:27–30; 7:29, 34; 15:1; 18:10–13). Luke is the only Evangelist to include this event with Zacchaeus, so we should assume that this episode reinforces a handful of themes found in the Gospel and in the immediate context. Tax collectors were unpopular in the first century (as they are in any century!), making a living off taxing goods at ports and roads. These tax collectors paid the tribute ahead of time to Rome—in full—and then turned around and collected payment as they deemed fit. It's safe to say, then, that Zacchaeus was not well liked in his community.

Perhaps the oddest detail of the event is Luke's description of Zacchaeus's height. According to 19:3, he was "small in stature." The Evangelists typically don't divulge these sorts of physical details unless they are important to the narrative. Since Zacchaeus is short and has trouble seeing Jesus over the throng of people, he "climbed up into a sycamore tree" (19:4). Why does Luke go out of his way to

---

10 Green, *Gospel of Luke*, 608.

mention his height and record him climbing a tree? Perhaps Luke narrates his diminutive height because it symbolizes God exalting the lowly or "small in stature." At the beginning of 19:8, the Evangelist records yet another odd detail: during (or after) the meal with Jesus, "Zacchaeus stood." Could it be that the act of standing up refers to his subsequent exaltation?

But that is not all. The story of Zacchaeus echoes the parable of the Pharisee and the tax collector a few verses earlier in 18:9–14. There, the Pharisee grandstands, boasting in his works and thanking God that he is unlike "extortioners, unjust, adulterers, or even like this tax collector" (18:11). In stark contrast, the tax collector, knowing full well that he has nothing to offer God, cries out, "God, be merciful to me, a sinner!" (18:13). Luke 18:14 cycles back to the great reversal: "For everyone *who exalts* [*ho hypsōn*] himself *will be humbled* [*tapeinōthēsetai*], but *the one who humbles* [*ho tapeinōn*] himself *will be exalted* [*hypsōthēsetai*]." The wording here is strikingly similar to what we saw in 14:11. God exalts the repentant tax collector but humbles the legalistic Pharisee.

Zacchaeus, the "chief tax collector," identifies with the tax collector in the parable in 18:13–14. In 19:9 Jesus announces the result of Zacchaeus's exaltation: "he also is a son of Abraham." Becoming part of *true* Israel rests on the condition of one's heart, not ethnic descent. God curses those who cling to their ethnic descent for deliverance, but he blesses those who acknowledge their sin. Mary's prediction in 1:55 that God will be merciful to "Abraham and his offspring" is coming to fruition in a most unexpected manner—the salvation of a chief tax collector!

Exaltation of Jesus

The final section is the most important leg of our journey—the exaltation of the Son of Man to the Father's right hand. This discussion intersects with chapter 6 on the success of the Son of Man, so I encourage readers to consider that chapter in conjunction with this section. Before I examine Jesus's exaltation, let's first contemplate his humility.

Remember, the operative maxim in Luke's Gospel is the exaltation of the lowly and the dethroning of the proud.

Above I noted that Luke identifies Jesus as Yahweh incarnate in the birth narrative (see 1:43–44). If this connection is indeed valid, then Luke has already presented Jesus in an incredibly humble state, even before his birth. The Lord of creation dwells in heaven, sovereignly ruling over the cosmos. He is indeed "the Mighty One" (1:49 CSB). So Jesus left his heavenly abode, became human, and joined the created order. In the words of Paul, "though he [Christ] was in the form of God, [he] did not count equality with God a thing to be grasped, but emptied himself, by taking the form of a servant, being born in the likeness of men" (Phil. 2:6–7). The incarnation itself, then, is one of the greatest displays of Jesus's humility.

The Third Gospel goes out of its way to underscore Jesus's lowly condition. He was born in a manger or feeding trough and possibly in the animal's quarters of a relative's house (Luke 2:7).[11] Mary and Joseph, too, on account of their poverty, offer up a pair of doves for Mary's purification instead of a lamb (2:24; see Lev. 12:6–8). Throughout Jesus's career, he evinced a life of humility and service. This is especially true of Passion Week. At the Last Supper, Jesus corrects the brashness of the disciples when he states, "For who is the greater, one who reclines at table or one who serves? Is it not the one who reclines at table? But I am among you as the one who serves" (Luke 22:27). Though Luke doesn't record Jesus washing the disciples' feet, it's likely that Jesus does so at this juncture (see John 13:1–17). What type of servant is Jesus? He's the suffering servant of Isaiah—the one who would bear the guilt and sin of the covenant community. In Luke 22:37 Jesus quotes Isaiah 53:12: "For I tell you that this Scripture must be fulfilled in me: 'And he was numbered with the transgressors.' For what is written about me has its fulfillment." We would be wise to consider the immediate and broad context of this important quotation.

11 For the likelihood of Jesus's birth in the animal quarters of a relative's house, see David E. Garland, *Luke*, ZECNT (Grand Rapids, MI: Zondervan, 2011), 121.

Isaiah 53:12 summarizes a great deal of the fourth and final Servant Song in Isaiah 52:13–53:12 (see also Isa. 42:1–9; 49:1–6; 50:4–9). The beginning of the fourth song reads in the Septuagint,

> See, my servant shall understand,
>> and he *shall be exalted* [*hypsōthēsetai*]
>> and glorified exceedingly. (Isa. 52:13 NETS)

Notice that once again the language of exaltation crops up. Perhaps with the exception of the Psalms, the book of Isaiah develops the great reversal more than any other Old Testament book. Several passages in Isaiah are strikingly similar to what we find in Luke's Gospel:

> For the eyes of the Lord are *lofty* [*hypsēloi*], but man is *lowly*
>> [*tapeinos*],
>> and *the loftiness* [*to hypsos*] of men shall be brought *low*
>> [*tapeinōthēsetai*],
> and the Lord alone *will be exalted* [*hypsōthēsetai*] in that day.
> For the day of the Lord Sabaoth will be
>> against everyone who is insolent and haughty
>> and against everyone who is *lofty* [*hypsēlon*] and high,
>> and they *shall be humbled* [*tapeinōthēsontai*]. (Isa. 2:11–12
>> NETS)

> And every person *shall be humbled* [*tapeinōthēsetai*],
>> and *the loftiness* [*hypsos*] of men shall fall,
>> and the Lord alone *will be exalted* [*hypsōthēsetai*] on that day.
>> (Isa. 2:17 NETS)

> For behold, the Sovereign, the Lord Sabaoth,
>> will mightily confound the glorious ones,
> and *the lofty* [*hoi hypsēloi*] will be crushed in their insolence,
>> and *the lofty will be brought low* [*hoi hypsēloi tapeinōthēsontai*].
>> (Isa. 10:33 NETS; cf. 25:12; 26:5)

These sections from Isaiah reveal God's judgment on the proud and idolatrous Israelites (Isa. 2:6–22; 25:12; 26:5) and the pagan nations (Isa. 10:33). Furthermore, the exaltation of the servant figure in Isaiah 52:13 should be understood within the larger context of Isaiah. At times, Isaiah describes God raising up or exalting specific individuals (e.g., Isa. 1:2; 4:2). But their exaltation qualitatively differs from Yahweh's exaltation or state of "sitting on a throne, *lofty* [*hypsēlou*] and raised up" (Isa. 6:1 NETS; cf. 12:5–6; 33:5, 10; 35:2; 57:15). Could it be that the exaltation of Isaiah's suffering servant in 52:13, though, has in mind the exaltation of Yahweh? Perhaps the two figures, Yahweh and the suffering servant, *are one and the same*. If the prophet Isaiah intends on bringing the two together, then there's no better place in the entire Old Testament for Luke to draw from. The Lord who rules over the cosmos is also the Lord who serves his people.

Luke is the only Evangelist to record Jesus's ascension. But he narrates the event twice—at the end of his Gospel in Luke 24:50–53 and again in Acts 1:9–11. Whereas John's Gospel views the cross as Jesus's exaltation (see John 3:14; 8:28; 12:32), Luke emphasizes Jesus's ascension as his exaltation. The whole of Jesus's career anticipates the ascension. Mary's words—"he has brought down the mighty from their thrones and exalted those of humble estate" (Luke 1:52)—ultimately refer to Jesus's ascension into heaven. As Jesus turns south toward Jerusalem, Luke comments, "When the days drew near for him *to be taken up*, he set his face to go to Jerusalem" (Luke 9:51). The goal, then, is Jesus's exaltation in his return to the Father.

I could say much about these thick passages, but only a few observations on Luke 24:51 and Acts 1:9 are in order:

While he blessed them, he parted from them and was carried up into heaven. (Luke 24:51)

And when he had said these things, as they were looking on, he was lifted up, and a cloud took him out of their sight. (Acts 1:9)

First, Jesus's ascension to heaven stands in stark contrast to Satan's fall from heaven (Luke 10:18). The two figures stand antithetical to one another. God dethrones Satan and exalts his Son. Second, the passive verbs "was carried" (Luke 24:51) and "was lifted up" (Acts 1:9) are a bit puzzling. Who's the implied agent? The Spirit? The Father? Thankfully, Acts 1:9 answers this question: "a cloud took him." The cloud here most likely refers to the Father, as Luke identifies him with a cloud earlier in Luke 9:34–35. Third, since Jesus is escorted to heaven in a cloud, we should connect his ascension to the programmatic prophecy of Daniel 7:13–14:

> with the clouds of heaven
>> there came one like *a son of man*,
> and he came to the Ancient of Days
>> and was presented before him.
> And to him was given dominion
>> and glory and a kingdom.

According to Daniel 7, the Ancient of Days grants the Son of Man the authority to govern the cosmos on account of his apparent defeat of the fourth beast (Dan. 7:11–12; cf. Ps. 110). The ascension, then, is the Father's cosmic declaration that his Son has successfully achieved the goal set before him and is now qualified to rule over all things (see Heb. 1:3–14; Rev. 5:1–14).

Jesus's faithful life, atoning death, and life-giving resurrection—the very heart of the gospel—while necessary in securing redemption, are not the climax. When Jesus ascends into heaven and sits down on his Father's throne, *then* he is qualified to carry out divine judgment on evil, initiate the new creation, serve as mediator between God and humanity, dwell with creation, pour forth the Spirit, and so on. Certainly, Jesus performs each of these elements during his earthly ministry, but his death, resurrection, and ascension to the Father's throne enables him to do so in a heightened or escalated manner.

Conclusion

Mary's prophecy that God would bring down rulers but exalt the humble is one of the most salient themes in Luke's Gospel, striking at the heart of Jesus's ministry. Luke appears to develop two strands of humiliation and exaltation—the humiliation of Satan and of those in alliance with him, and the exaltation of Jesus's followers and of Jesus himself. Jesus's humility precipitates his exaltation. Jesus is exalted to the right hand of his Father, a status that only God himself enjoys. Believers are also exalted but not to the Father's throne, for their exaltation is in the veritable presence of God. Believers rule on behalf of God; they do not rule as God. Juxtaposed with Christ's humiliation and subsequent exaltation is Satan. Satan's self-acclaimed exalted state, his hubris, leads to his eventual demise. Those exalted rulers who oppress God's people and embody Satan's boastful attitude will be cut down as well.

The church would do well to choose the path of humiliation that leads to exaltation. A friend of mine once told me, "For believers, this is the worst life can get. For unbelievers, this is the best life can get." This proverb captures the conflicting worldviews of the church and the world. The world chases fame and adulation, whereas true believers pursue service and Christ's honor. Unbelievers temporarily live in an exalted state. When Christ returns, though, unbelievers will be made low in eternal judgment. Believers, on the other hand, enjoy a state of humiliation in the present, as the world does its worst to us. But, at the second coming, Christ will escort us into the new creation where we will reign for all of eternity.

Peace on Earth and in Heaven

PEACE IS A SALIENT AND UNIQUE FEATURE of the Third Gospel. The word for "peace" (*eirēnē*) occurs a total of twenty-five times in the Gospels, and fourteen of those occurrences are in Luke. Furthermore, the term is found on three significant occasions (see table 2.1).

Table 2.1   Announcements of Peace in Luke

Reference	Speaker and Occasion
Luke 2:14: "Glory to God in the highest, and *on earth peace* among those with whom he is pleased!"	Angels at Jesus's birth
Luke 19:38: "Blessed is the King who comes in the name of the Lord! *Peace in heaven* and glory in the highest!"	Pilgrims at Jesus's triumphal entry
Luke 24:36: "As they were talking about these things, Jesus himself stood among them, and said to them, '*Peace to you!*'"	Jesus to his disciples after his resurrection

Notice that the first and second announcements specify *where* peace is found. In 2:14 the angels proclaim peace "on earth," and in 19:38 the pilgrims declare peace "in heaven." Clearly, Luke wants his readers to bring both passages together. Juxtaposing "earth" (*gē*) and "heaven" (*ouranos*) is a common way to refer to the totality of the cosmos—all physical and spiritual realities.[1] The point, then, is that Jesus's ministry, from beginning to end, is the pursuit of end-time cosmic peace.

This chapter unpacks Luke's concern to present Jesus as the one who offers peace to the universe with a focus on these three texts (2:14; 19:38; 24:36). But before I examine them, I will first paint in broad brushstrokes a biblical theology of cosmic unity. Why is peace needed on earth *and* in heaven? How will this peace be achieved? And what is the result of cosmic peace? Jesus's life, death, and resurrection unify a broken cosmos, so that humanity and creation may enjoy God's glory.

Created to Rule over the Serpent

According to Genesis 3:1, "The serpent was more crafty than any other beast of the field *that the LORD God had made.*" And in Genesis 1:1, God "created the heavens and the earth," an expression that includes angelic beings. So if we read between the lines, God created Satan, the serpent, between Genesis 1:1 and 1:2. The angelic rebellion must have also occurred in this interval. In any case, the point is that spiritual hostility existed between God / his angelic cohort and rebellious angels before the fall of humanity. Also, because God made the serpent, he is sovereign over it (and the other rebellious angels).

By associating the serpent with creation, the implication is that Adam and Eve, created in God's image, were tasked with ruling over the serpent (see Gen. 1:26–28; 2:15). As kings representing God on earth, Adam and Eve should have quickly subdued the serpent, a ghastly unclean animal (see Lev. 11; Deut. 14). They should have prevented the serpent from slithering into Eden in the first place or at least have evicted it when it arrived! If we read between the lines once more, it is possible to conclude that the first couple had let their guard down and were not proactively warding off unclean

---

1   See, e.g., (LXX for Old Testmaent texts) Gen. 1:1; 2:1, 4; 24:7; Pss. 8:2; 56:12; Isa. 37:16; Matt. 5:18; 11:25; Luke 10:21; 16:17; 21:33; Eph. 1:10; Rev. 21:1.

animals. Jeffrey Niehaus keenly observes, "The presence of the foe [in the garden] presents the human with an opportunity to wage war."[2] Such a reading of Genesis 1–3 explains King David's declaration in Psalm 8:5–6 (8:6–7 MT / LXX):

> Yet you have made him [Adam] a *little* [MT: *me'at*; LXX: *brachy ti*] lower than *the heavenly beings* [MT: *elohim*; LXX: *angelous*]
> and crowned him with glory and honor.
> You have given him dominion over the works of your hands;
> you have put all things under his feet.

This psalm brilliantly looks back at Adam's failure in the garden in Genesis 1–3 and, simultaneously, looks forward to what a coming Adam figure will achieve at the end of history (see 1 Cor. 15:27; Eph. 1:22). God created Adam "a little lower" than "heavenly beings" or "angels." While the Hebrew word *elohim* in Psalm 8:5 (8:6 MT) may refer to God, the Greek translator(s) clearly renders it as a reference to angels. Furthermore, and critical to our line of interpretation, the adjective "little" may not refer to the quality or degree (i.e., God made Adam a *little* lower than the angels) but to a temporary arrangement (i.e., God made Adam lower than the angels *for a little while*). When the author of Hebrews quotes this precise section of Psalm 8 in Hebrews 2:7–8, it appears that he understands "little" in a temporal sense (see CSB; ESV; NASB; NLT).

What difference does Psalm 8:5–6 make in understanding the nature of angels and God's plan for humanity? If we read Genesis 1–3 in light of Psalm 8:5–6, then we conclude that God expected Adam to rule over the serpent (who represents all rebellious angels), so that God would subsequently "put all things under his feet." In other words, Psalm 8 is one of the clearest texts in the Old Testament that

---

2   Jeffrey J. Niehaus, *The Common Grace Covenants*, vol. 1 of *Biblical Theology* (Wooster, OH: Weaver, 2014), 103.

weds humans, created in the image of God, with ruling over the angelic realm. It would also explain why Paul enigmatically declares, "Do you not know that we are to judge angels?" (1 Cor. 6:3).[3]

The Fragmentation and Restructuring of God's People

Because Adam and Eve failed to secure their authority over the serpent, the serpent ruled over them. One salient result of the serpent ruling over the original couple is his prerogative to fracture humanity from God and from one another. This becomes clear in Genesis 3:15 and the famous war of the seeds: "I will put enmity between you [the serpent] and the woman, and between your offspring and her offspring." Soon after this promise, Cain kills his brother Abel (Gen. 4:8), so God exiles Cain from his divine presence (Gen. 4:12, 14, 16). Hostility between the godly and ungodly lines culminates in the flood of judgment that God executes on the unrighteous (Gen. 6:5–8, 11–12). Once the flood waters recede, Noah's sons—Shem, Ham, and Japheth—form the next phase of the covenant community (Gen. 10). Instead of multiplying and spreading out to the four corners of the earth in obedience to Genesis 1:28, the descendants of these three sons, seventy nations total, gather at Shinar where they set out to build "a city and a tower with its top in the heavens" so that they can "make a name for [themselves]" (Gen. 11:4). God, as a result of their disobedience, promised to "confuse their language," and then he "dispersed them from there over the face of all the earth" (Gen. 11:7–8). God divides humanity into seventy nations—the LXX reads seventy-two—each with its own language, culture, and identity.

According to the Old Testament (and Second Temple Judaism), God appointed angels in Genesis 11 to rule over the nations on his behalf. We discern this phenomenon in Deuteronomy 32:8:

---

3   Meredith Kline likewise comments on Adam's royal authority in Eden, "The hope was held out to man to become participant in that realm of the heavenly council which was the primal domain of the Lord God within his creation" (*Kingdom Prologue: Genesis Foundations for a Covenantal Worldview* [Eugene, OR: Wipf & Stock, 2006], 46).

When the Most High gave to the nations their inheritance,
>   when he divided mankind,
> he fixed the borders of the peoples
>   according to the number of the sons of God.[4]

The last phrase of this verse is notoriously difficult to pin down, but most Septuagint manuscripts prefer the reading, "according to the number of the angels of God" (*kata arithmon angelōn theou*). An early Jewish commentary, the Targum, on Deuteronomy 32:8 (Pseudo-Jonathan) is explicit:

> When the Most High gave the world as an inheritance to the nations who had come out of the children of Noah, when He had set aside their writing systems and their languages to mankind in the generation of the division, in which time He cast lots with the seventy angels, the princes of the nations with whom he had been revealed with them to see the city, and in which time he established the borders of the nations according to the number of the seventy souls of Israel who went down to Egypt.[5]

Apparently, these angelic overseers were to report to God and manage the nations' affairs by keeping them separate from one another. Israel, on the other hand, did not have a patron "deity" acting on behalf of God.[6] He enjoyed had an intimate relationship with Israel and did not require a mediatorial ruler. Instead of ruling well on God's behalf,

---

4   The MT reads "sons of Israel" (*bene yisra'el*) along with a handful of LXX recensions (Aquila, Symmachus, and Theodotion). Most LXX manuscripts, though, contain "according to the number of the angels of God" (*kata arithmon angelōn theou*; see also 4QDeut). For the likelihood of the latter reading, see Michael S. Heiser, "Deuternonomy 32:8 and the Sons of God," *BibSac* 158, no. 629 (2001): 52–74.

5   Translation of Targum Pseudo-Jonathan by Eldon Clem (OakTree Software, 2015).

6   See Daniel Block, *The Gods of the Nations: Studies in Ancient Near Eastern National Theology*, 2nd ed. (Grand Rapids, MI: Baker, 2000); G. B. Caird, *New Testament Theology*, completed and ed. L. D. Hurst (Oxford: Clarendon, 1995), 102–3; M. Heiser, *The Unseen Realm: Recovering the Supernatural Worldview of the Bible* (Bellingham, WA: Lexham, 2019), 113–15.

the angels perverted their God-given authority and sought power by attempting to be the source of power and authority (Ps. 82; cf. Deut. 4:19; Judg. 11:24; Acts 17:26).

In this regard, the apocalyptic book of Daniel contains some of the most developed and intriguing insights into the relationship between angels and their corresponding nations. The archangel Gabriel, the protector of Israel (Dan. 8:16; 9:21; cf. 6:22; Job 33:23–26), tells the prophet Daniel, "The prince of the kingdom of Persia withstood me twenty-one days, but Michael, one of the chief princes, came to help me" (Dan. 10:13). Then, a handful of verses later, he states, "But now I will return to fight against the prince of Persia; and when I go out, behold, the prince of Greece will come. . . . There is none who contends by my side against these except Michael, your prince" (Dan. 10:20–21). Along these lines, earlier in the book of Daniel, a ruler or "little horn . . . grew as high as the heavenly army [angels], made some of the army and some of the stars fall to the earth, and trampled them" (Dan. 8:9–10 CSB). Three critical and enigmatic principles emerge from these passages: (1) in line with our previous contention, the book of Daniel affirms that angels represent pagan nations—namely, "the prince of Persia" and "the prince of Greece"; (2) these representative angels wage a cosmic battle against God's archangels and other heavenly beings;[7] (3) there appears to be a hierarchy of righteous and unrighteous angels (see also Tob. 12:15; 1 En. 9:1).

In addition to fighting a spiritual war in the heavens, these malevolent angels drove a deeper wedge between the earthly nations by promoting idolatry and false religion. This explains why idolatry and demons are often found together. According to Paul, a demon stands behind every idol: "What pagans sacrifice they offer to demons and not to God" (1 Cor. 10:20; see also Lev. 17:7; Deut. 32:17; Ps. 90:6 [LXX]; Bar. 4:7).

The overall point should not be missed: as a result of humanity's sin, God split humanity into distinct people groups and commissioned

---

7   Cf. 1QM XII, 4–9; XIII, 1–2; XV, 13–17.

angels to rule over them. But the rebellious angels failed and enticed the nations to commit idolatry.[8] Furthermore, these representative angels also fight against righteous angels. Demons, division, idolatry, and cosmic warfare form a deep nexus of wickedness and rebellion.

Division and rebellion would not prevail though. The Old Testament yearns for the day when the entire cosmos is reconciled to God. A robust view of peace and reconciliation is multifaceted, as it entails a restoration of humanity's relationship with God, a restoration of people groups with one another, and, implicitly, a subjugation of all hostile angelic forces.

The Old Testament locates God's great act of reconciliation at the end of history—in the "latter days." Eschatological reconciliation primarily concerns God reconciling a rebellious and unholy humanity to himself (e.g., Isa. 53:3; Ezek. 45:15, 17; Dan. 9:24). When God draws humanity to himself, he also promises to break down the barriers between people groups. Vertical reconciliation *results* in horizontal reconciliation (e.g., Isa. 2:3; 56:3–8; 57:14–19; 66:18–21; Zech. 2:11; 8:20–23). Humanity must first fellowship with God before fellowship with one another is possible.

God also promises to restore harmony within the created environment in the end times. For example, Isaiah 65:25 reads,

> The wolf and the lamb shall graze together;
>   the lion shall eat straw like the ox,
>   and dust shall be the serpent's food.
> They shall not hurt or destroy
>   in all my holy mountain.

While the Old Testament does not explicitly address the issue of angelic reconciliation, it may be a legitimate inference. We even catch a glimmer of this notion in the Theodotion translation of Daniel 7:14 (NETS):

---

8   Rebellious angels, the "Watchers," leading humanity to idolatry is explicitly developed in 1 En. 1–36, an early Jewish work known as the Book of Watchers (see also Jub. 10:1–13).

"And to him [the son of man] was given the *dominion* [*hē archē*] and the honor and the kingship." According to Daniel 10, the angel Gabriel informs Daniel that the "ruler of the kingdom of the Persians" fought against the archangel Michael (10:13 NETS). A few verses later, Gabriel goes on to state that he will "fight against *the ruler* [*archontos*] of the Persians" and that the "*ruler* [*ho archōn*] of the Greeks was coming" (10:20 NETS). If we read Daniel 7:14 alongside Daniel 10, then the son of man's rule is not merely earthly but also heavenly. He rules over all things physical and spiritual. Angelic reconciliation, then, is not presented in salvific terms (i.e., demons repent and are converted); rather, the reconciliation of hostile angels entails submission to God and the son of man's reign (cf. Col. 1:20). This comes admirably close to our interpretation of Psalm 8, where God created Adam to rule over physical and spiritual realities.

"Peace on Earth" (2:14)

Since we've canvassed some of the contours of angels and their relationship to Israel and the surrounding nations, we can better understand Luke's emphasis on the matter. Our investigation begins with one of the most familiar passages in all of Christendom:

> And in the same region there were shepherds out in the field, keeping watch over their flock by night. And *an angel of the Lord* appeared to them, and the *glory of the Lord shone around them*, and they were filled with great fear. And the angel said to them, "Fear not, for behold, I bring you good news of great joy that will be for all the people. For unto you is born this day in the city of David a Savior, who is Christ the Lord. And this will be a sign for you: you will find a baby wrapped in swaddling cloths and lying in a manger." And suddenly there was with the angel *a multitude of the heavenly host* praising God and saying,
>
> > "Glory to God in the highest,
> >   and on earth peace among those with whom he is pleased!"

When the angels went away from them into heaven, the shepherds said to one another, "Let us go over to Bethlehem and see this thing that has happened, which the Lord has made known to us." (2:8–15)

Much could be said about this rich passage, but I will focus my attention on Luke's emphasis on the angels at the birth of Christ. Luke has already used the description "angel of the Lord" (2:9) as a reference to the archangel Gabriel, who appeared to Zechariah and Mary in 1:11–20 and 1:26–38.[9] Most likely, then, we should assume that it is Gabriel who visits the shepherds in the field (2:9–12). We noticed above that the archangel Gabriel appears in Daniel 8:16 and 9:21, where he interprets Daniel's vision. The angel in Daniel 10, while not explicitly identified, is most likely Gabriel. According to Daniel 10, Gabriel takes on a military role as the "prince of the kingdom of Persia," an evil angel, resists him; the archangel Michael then comes to Gabriel's aid (Dan. 10:13). An early Jewish work, the War Scroll at Qumran, even lists his name on some of the shields used in the final eschatological battle.[10]

Perhaps the most dramatic detail to this passage is Luke's description of other angels who abruptly arrive on the scene: "And suddenly there was with the angel a multitude *of the heavenly host* [*stratias ouraniou*]" (Luke 2:13). The term for "host" (*stratia*) clearly connotes a military dimension,[11] and on a few occasions angels are associated with such a "host."[12] But the clearest Old Testament background lies in several texts in the LXX that use the identical wording—"heavenly host"—to refer to angels who stand before the presence of God in heaven and serve in the divine council. For example, 1 Kings 22:19 / 3 Reigns 22:19 (NETS)

9   1QM IX.14–18; cf. 4Q529 1, 2–4. Raymond Brown rightly observes that "in [Luke's] description of Gabriel's appearance Luke intends to evoke the atmosphere of Daniel" (*The Birth of the Messiah: A Commentary on the Infancy Narratives of Matthew and Luke* [Garden City, NY: Image, 1979], 270).

10   See J. J. Collins, "Gabriel," in *Dictionary of Deities and Demons in the Bible*, ed. Karel van der Toorn, Bob Becking, and Pieter W. van der Horst (Grand Rapids, MI: Eerdmans, 1999), 338–39.

11   See, e.g., LXX Ex. 14:4; Num. 10:28; Deut. 20:9; Judg. 8:6; 1 Macc. 2:66.

12   Rev. Ezra 6:16; LAE 38:3; 4 Macc. 4:10; Josephus, *J.W.* 5.388.

states, "I saw the Lord God of Israel, sitting on his throne, and *all the host of heaven* [*pasa hē stratia tou ouranou*] stood near him on his right and on his left." Again, Nehemiah 9:6 / 2 Esdras 19:6 (NETS) reads, "You yourself are the Lord alone . . . *the armies of the heavens* [*hai stratiai tōn ouranōn*] do obeisance to you" (see also LXX of 2 Chron. 33:3, 5; Jer. 7:18; 8:2; 19:13; Hos. 13:4; Zeph. 1:5; cf. Acts 7:42). But why would Luke color this passage with military overtones? Luke presents angels as mighty warriors preparing for battle. Their mighty, divine King has arrived, and *because they are convinced that he will win the battle, they announce his success well before he begins to fight.*

Luke mentions in 2:1 that Jesus was born during the reign of Caesar Augustus (27 BC–AD 14), who established the famous Pax Romana ("Roman Peace") throughout the empire. In contrast to the chaotic decades that preceded his rule, Augustus promised internal stability within his own government and abroad. Order, stability, and peace were the goals. But the peace that the angels announce at the birth of Jesus is far more comprehensive. The Pax Romana was only skin deep, touched some of Rome's neighbors, and lasted a few hundred years. The peace that Jesus establishes penetrates human hearts, reaches the far corners of the universe, and will never end.

One final dimension of this text is worth pursuing, albeit in brief. The angels first declare that peace is found "on earth," and then they further specify *where* on earth—"among those with whom [God] *is pleased* [*eudokias*]" (Luke 2:14). Another text in Luke's Gospel mentions God showing favor: Jesus's baptism in 3:21–22. There we read, "A voice came from heaven, 'You are my beloved Son, with you I *am well pleased* [*eudokēsa*]'" (3:22). The two texts must be related at some level. Jesus was, of course, never estranged from his Father, so he never needed his Father's redemptive and salvific peace. But it may be that the baptism is an outward, public display of peace/favor that the Father reveals to those gathered at the Jordan. So as Jesus ministers throughout Galilee and Jerusalem, all those who trust in Jesus likewise identify with God's peace/favor. God extends them peace/favor because he has already shown his Son peace/favor (cf. 12:32; Matt. 12:18; 17:5).

"Peace in Heaven" (19:38)

The next passage to discuss (Luke 19:38) describes an event that occurs at the triumphal entry:

> As he was drawing near—already on the way down the Mount of Olives—the whole multitude of his disciples began to rejoice and praise God with a loud voice for all the mighty works that they had seen, saying, "Blessed is the King who comes in the name of the Lord! *Peace in heaven [en ouranō eirēnē]* and glory in the highest!" (19:37–38)

The occasion is Sunday of Passion Week, and Jesus has finished his trek to Jerusalem, a journey that began some ten chapters earlier in Luke's Gospel (9:51). Why do the pilgrims cry out, "Peace in heaven and glory in the highest"? All four Gospels record the triumphal entry, and only Luke mentions "peace in heaven" (see table 2.2).

Table 2.2   The Triumphal Entry in the Gospels

Matthew 21:9	Mark 11:9–10	Luke 19:37–38	John 12:13
"And the crowds that went before him and that followed him were shouting, 'Hosanna to the Son of David! Blessed is he who comes in the name of the Lord! Hosanna in the highest!'"	"And those who went before and those who followed were shouting, 'Hosanna! Blessed is he who comes in the name of the Lord! Blessed is the coming kingdom of our father David! Hosanna in the highest!'"	"The whole multitude of his disciples began to rejoice and praise God with a loud voice for all the mighty works that they had seen, saying, 'Blessed is the King who comes in the name of the Lord! *Peace in heaven and glory in the highest!*'"	"So they took branches of palm trees and went out to meet him, crying out, 'Hosanna! Blessed is he who comes in the name of the Lord, even the King of Israel!'"

Josephus, a first-century Jewish historian, claimed that around three million visitors flocked to Jerusalem to celebrate Passover (*J. W.* 2.280;

6.425).[13] Many scholars today, though, believe that the actual number was approximately two or three hundred thousand.[14] The bustling crowd that gathers around Jesus as he rides on the donkey soon causes a commotion. These people are arriving into town on Sunday to celebrate Passover that Friday, as it was common to arrive a week early. The pilgrims quote Psalm 118:26 (Luke 19:38), a line from a collection of psalms called the Psalms of Hallel (Pss. 104–6; 120–36; 146–50). Pilgrims would sing these psalms during the Feast of Tabernacles, Pentecost, and the first day of Passover. The Psalms of Hallel also bear the name "Egyptian Hallel" because they recall Israel's exodus from Egypt and because they anticipate a second, greater redemption. When these pilgrims witness Jesus's symbolic gesture of riding on a donkey, clearly demonstrating his messianic identity (see Zech. 9:9; Matt. 21:1–5), they are likely convinced that Jesus will ascend the throne of David immediately and cast off the weighty yoke of Rome.

But why do the pilgrims oddly mention "peace in heaven"? The phrase seems incongruent with the triumphal entry, an event that takes place *on earth* in Jerusalem. I. Howard Marshall is right to comment, "To speak of peace in heaven is unusual."[15] Solving this riddle requires us to flip back to an earlier passage in Luke's narrative, where Jesus "saw Satan fall like lightning *from heaven* [*ek tou ouranou*]" (Luke 10:18). Satan, the great accuser of God's people, initially lost his position of authority on account of Jesus's success in the wilderness temptation (see chapter 6). Peace in heaven is directly tied to the devil's success in the garden. Instead of Adam and Eve ruling over the devil, he ruled over them and gained a foothold over the cosmos, particularly in separating humanity and seducing them into idolatry. The immediate context of Luke 10 affirms this suggestion.

---

13   This paragraph excerpted and adapted from page 170 of *Handbook on the Gospels* by Benjamin L. Gladd, copyright © 2021. Used by permission of Baker Academic, a division of Baker Publishing Group.

14   E.g., Eckhard J. Schnabel, *Jesus in Jerusalem: The Last Days* (Grand Rapids, MI: Eerdmans, 2018), 157.

15   *The Gospel of Luke: A Commentary on the Greek Text*, NIGTC (Grand Rapids, MI: Eerdmans, 1978), 715.

At the beginning of the chapter, Jesus commissions seventy-two disciples[16] to proclaim the arrival of God's kingdom (Luke 10:1–12). Why
seventy-two? Commentators often argue that the seventy-two disciples
evoke the seventy-two people groups in Genesis 10, recalling Jesus's
"mission to all the nations of the earth."[17] This passage in Luke 10 is
not a far cry from Luke's list of diaspora Jews in Acts 2:9–11, a text that
also alludes to the Table of Nations in Genesis 10. The prominence of
Genesis 10 in both Luke 10 and Acts 2 indicates that Luke is well aware
of the Genesis narrative as he carefully weaves it into his two-volume
project. It may not be a matter of speculation, then, to suggest a connection between Satan's fall in Luke 10:18 and the Table of Nations /
Babel narrative in Genesis 10–11. I discussed the prominence of Satan's
downfall in chapter 1 and noticed how Luke 10:18–20 fits into Luke's
wider aim in "the great reversal." In light of our conclusion above that
God separated humanity into seventy nations and appointed an angelic
overseer to manage their affairs, Luke's reference to Satan in 10:18
makes brilliant sense. When Satan and the other malevolent angels fell
from heaven because of Christ's work at the temptation (and further at
the cross and resurrection), they positionally lost their authority over
the nations. Humanity is no longer shackled to rebellious angels. This
sequence of events opens the door for the gospel to take root among
the nations. To state the matter differently, the salvation of the Gentiles
is due, at least in part, to Jesus's victory over demons.

Notice, too, that at the beginning of Luke 10, Jesus charges the
seventy-two disciples to proclaim "peace" to each house they enter:

---

16 The LXX includes seventy-two nations in the list in Gen. 10:2–31, but the MT contains
seventy. This divergence probably explains why some manuscripts in Luke 10:1 read
"seventy" (א A C L W Θ) and others read "seventy-two" (𝔓⁷⁵ B D 33). Deciding which
variant is correct is notoriously tricky because both readings are supported early and
have wide attestation. But for our purposes, the textual issue in Luke 10:1 reinforces the
allusion to Gen. 10–11.

17 John Nolland, *Luke 9:21–18:34*, WBC (Grand Rapids, MI: Zondervan, 1993), 549. See also
David E. Garland, *Luke*, ZECNT (Grand Rapids, MI: Zondervan, 2011), 425; François
Bovon, *Luke 2: A Commentary on the Gospel of Luke 9:51–19:27*, trans. Donald S. Deer,
Hermeneia (Minneapolis: Fortress, 2007), 26.

Whatever house you enter, first say, "*Peace* be to this house!" And if a *son of peace* is there, your peace will rest upon him. But if not, it will return to you. And remain in the same house, eating and drinking what they provide, for the laborer deserves his wages. Do not go from house to house. (10:5–7)

This is not a generic type of peace that the disciples herald. It's a peace tied to the inauguration of the kingdom and may even be synonymous with it in this text (10:8–12; cf. Acts 10:36). *Because* the seventy-two disciples are successful in announcing the eternal kingdom (Luke 10:17), the kingdom is expanding through their ministry. The kingdom of Satan is continuing to crumble, and the ministry of the seventy-two disciples is so successful that its effects ripple throughout the spiritual realm, prompting Jesus to exclaim, "I saw Satan fall like lighting" (10:18).

While the mission of seventy-two disciples in Luke 10 appears to be confined to Palestine (see 10:13–15), their ministry foreshadows the gospel going forth to the nations. Therefore, the pilgrims' declaration that there is "peace in heaven" at the triumphal entry acknowledges, at least from the narrative's perspective, Jesus's defeat of all inimical forces in the spiritual realm. What took place in the wilderness temptation is further actualized in the sending out of the seventy-two disciples and at the cross and resurrection. The advancement of the kingdom promotes peace and reconciliation.

"Peace to You" (24:36)

The final leg in our journey is Jesus's post-resurrection appearance with the disciples: "As they were talking about these things, Jesus himself stood among them, and said to them, 'Peace to you!'" (Luke 24:36 // John 20:19, 21, 26). This is the first time in Luke's account when Jesus explicitly grants "peace" to his disciples. Earlier, he granted peace to the woman who anointed him with oil (Luke 7:50) and to the woman with an issue of blood (8:48). Luke 2:14 is critical to capturing the thrust of Jesus's words to his disciples: "Glory to God in the highest, and on earth *peace among those with whom he is pleased*!" Aligning

2:14 with 24:36, I conclude that God is now "pleased" or has "shown favor" on the disciples. Furthermore, as an aside, note that in 2:14 God is the one showing favor, whereas in 24:36 Jesus shows favor. Jesus does what God does. But why has it taken so long for Jesus to grant peace to his disciples? The answer lies in the immediate context in which the disciples are finally grasping the contours of Jesus's identity.

After Jesus rose from the dead and the women discovered the vacant tomb and two attending angels (24:1–8), the women reported to the eleven disciples and a handful of other followers what they learned. But the disciples "did not believe" the women (24:11). Luke then recounts the journey of two of these other followers (Cleopas and an unnamed disciple). Jesus joins these two individuals on the road to Emmaus and castigates them for being "slow of heart to believe all that the prophets have spoken" (24:25). Jesus then proceeds to walk them through the bulk of the Old Testament, showing them how Israel's Scriptures anticipate him.

Later that day, the two disciples meet with "the eleven and those who were with them" (24:33). Although Luke doesn't include this event, the eleven disciples inform the two disciples that Jesus "has appeared to Simon" (24:34; cf. 1 Cor 15:5). Then Jesus supernaturally appears in their midst and announces, "Peace to you" (Luke 24:36). Immediately before explaining to the disciples that the Old Testament indeed predicts his death and resurrection, he "opened their minds to understand the Scriptures" (24:45). A correct understanding of the Old Testament and its relationship to Jesus is ultimately a gift from God.

Luke fast-forwards to the ascension, an event that takes place on the Mount of Olives, and describes Jesus's final act: ". . . lifting up his hands he blessed them. . . . And [the disciples] worshiped him" (24:50, 52). As some scholars point out, this gesture is highly reminiscent of Leviticus 9:22 when the high priest, Aaron, "lifted up his hands toward the people and blessed them."[18] But these scholars often miss a critical piece to this Leviticus 9:22 allusion. Following the blessing of Moses

---

18 See, e.g., John Nolland, *Luke 18:35–24:53*, WBC (Grand Rapids, MI: Zondervan, 1993), 1227.

and Aaron, *"the glory of the* LORD *appeared to all the people. And fire came out from before the* LORD *and consumed the burnt offering and the pieces of fat on the altar, and when all the people saw it, they shouted and fell on their faces"* (Lev. 9:23–24). Blessing in the Old Testament is always tied, in some fashion, to God's life-giving presence.

Jesus declaring "peace" to the disciples in Luke 24:36 and then "blessing" them at his ascension in 24:50 speak volumes. The two acts must be related. If I am correct in my previous appraisal of Luke's presentation of "peace" in his Gospel, then the implication is clear: Jesus's obedient life, death, and resurrection unified the spiritual and earthly realms. Now that the Father has put all of creation under the sovereign control of the Son, God's glorious presence and his eternal kingdom can be established. This principle is precisely the reason why God chose Solomon to build the temple and not David. First Kings 5:3–4 repeats Solomon's desire to build a temple: "You know that David my father could not build a house for the name of the LORD his God because of the warfare with which his enemies surrounded him, *until the* LORD *put them under the soles of his feet.* But now the LORD my *God has given me rest on every side."* David is a "man of war" (1 Chron. 28:3; cf. 22:8), whereas Solomon is a man of peace. Peace must be achieved before God can dwell intimately with his people (see also Josh. 1:13–15; 11:23; 21:44; 23:1–4). The entire point, then, of Jesus bringing peace to the universe is for God to dwell intimately with the created order.

Conclusion

The effect of Jesus securing peace in heaven and on earth is threefold: (1) the physical and spiritual realms are now in subjection to Christ. While the spiritual realm is cognizant of this reality—that is, even the demons acknowledge Jesus's superiority (e.g., Luke 4:34; 8:28)—the majority of the physical realm does not (e.g., pagan rulers). (2) Cosmic peace brings unity to both realms. Here the physical realm comes to the fore. The strained relationships between the various people groups that characterized humanity before the coming of Christ has been overcome. Christ has defeated these rebellious angels who stood behind the idolatrous nations. The nations now identify solely with Jesus, the true Israel of God. All of humanity, Jews and Gentiles, enjoy complete solidarity with one another through Christ. (3) Now that Jesus has procured cosmic peace, God can establish his kingdom and his presence among his people. Kingdom and temple are not synonyms, yet they are organically related. God fills the kingdom with his glory.

Believers can be confident that Satan and his malevolent allies cannot dislodge them from Christ's grip (Rom. 8:38–39). Christ's victory is the church's victory. And since believers reign with him and enjoy the life-giving presence of the Spirit, they are empowered to pursue righteousness and peace with one another.

3

Israel, the Gentiles, and
Isaiah's Servant

SIMEON PROPHESIES OVER BABY JESUS in the Nunc Dimittis (Luke 2:29–32), establishing themes that color all of Luke-Acts. He alludes to Isaiah 49:6, one of the most prominent passages in the book of Isaiah, when he exclaims that Jesus will be a "light for revelation to the Gentiles" (Luke 2:32). According to Isaiah 49:1–7, the famed servant figure is true Israel who restores the remnant of Israelites. But God also charges the servant with converting the nations. Luke even alludes to Isaiah 49:6 in the programmatic verse of Acts 1:8 and later quotes the same passage in Paul's first missionary journey, as the apostle shifts his focus to sharing the gospel with the nations (Acts 13:47). Clearly, then, Jesus's identity as the Isaianic servant takes on special significance for the whole of Luke-Acts.

I will first explore how Luke presents Jesus as the long-awaited servant of Isaiah in order to explain Jesus's twofold mission: the restoration of a remnant of Israelites and the inclusion of the nations. While earlier portions of the Old Testament certainly anticipate these aims, the prophet Isaiah develops this twofold goal by isolating a single, faithful individual. All four Gospels certainly draw their readers' attention to the inclusion of the Gentiles into the people of God, but Luke develops this theme to an even greater degree, especially in the book of Acts.

Finally, once we get a handle on the incorporation of Gentiles into true Israel, we will then take a step back and consider the term *Israel* itself and what it means to participate in the covenant community in the person of Christ. Jews and Gentiles stand on equal footing on account of his identity and finished work.

Dedicated to the Lord

For us to appreciate the significance of Simeon's declaration that Jesus is the long-awaited servant of Isaiah (Luke 2:25–35), we must first examine why Mary and Joseph trek to Jerusalem in the first place (2:22–24). They arrive at the temple in Jerusalem with baby Jesus for two purposes: (1) the law dictates that a priest offer up a sacrifice for Mary's purification (see Lev. 12:6–8); (2) the couple must also dedicate Jesus to the Lord. Luke 2:23 loosely quotes Exodus 13:2, 12, and 15 to explain why Jesus's parents are compelled to dedicate Jesus.

According to Exodus 13:1–16, Moses instructs the Israelites to dedicate their firstborn and livestock. God ordained this important rite on account of the final plague poured out on the firstborn of Egypt and Israel (Ex. 12:12–13). Since he spared the firstborn Israelite males from destruction, God legally claims them as his own. Exodus 13:2 states, "Consecrate to me all the firstborn. Whatever is the first to open the womb among the people of Israel, both of man and of beast, is mine" (see also Ex. 22:29–30; Num. 3:13; 18:14–19). The firstborn males represent the entire family unit, and the firstborn livestock represent the entire herd or flock (cf. Ex. 4:22). By setting apart Jesus to God and declaring him "consecrated" or "holy" (*hagios*), Mary and Joseph affirm the truthfulness of Gabriel's prophecy that Jesus will be the "holy" one (*hagion*; Luke 1:35). So Luke encourages his readers to view Jesus not only as the firstborn of his immediate family but also as the firstborn of all of God's people (cf. Heb. 2:11–13). If Jesus is the firstborn of humanity, then we should expect that the salvation of the nations is central to his ministry.

Another layer of Jesus's consecration is still worth pursuing. Commentators often ignore the strong connection between Exodus 12 and 13. The dedication of the firstborn in Exodus 13 is predicated on what transpired in Exodus 12. Just as the firstborn represents the family, so also the Passover sacrifice, a lamb or goat, represents the family. Recall that each Israelite family dabbed the blood of the sacrifice around the entrance to the home (Ex. 12:7). God "passed over" those families who obeyed the ordinance by applying blood to the top of the door and to the door posts. But God executed judgment on those who failed to sacrifice a lamb or goat (12:29–30). A strong connection exists, then, between the sacrifice and God's people. The animal dies *on behalf of* the humans. The sacrificial system, though not formalized at a corporate level until God formally gives Moses the law (see, e.g., Ex. 29–30; Lev. 1–27), finds its point of origin in Genesis 3. In contrast to Adam and Eve's self-manufactured clothes (Gen. 3:7), an attempt to restore their inheritance and relationship with God on their own terms, God clothes the first couple with "garments of skins" (Gen. 3:21). Only an atoning sacrifice will do. Noah, Abraham, Isaac, and Jacob offered up animal sacrifices with some regularity. Moses, though, officially instituted various types of sacrifices that relate to the tabernacle/temple and the worshiper (see discussion in chapter 7).

Luke may broach the issue of consecration in Luke 2 because he wants to identify Jesus early in his narrative with the Passover lamb. When he and the disciples celebrate the Passover at the end of Passion Week, Jesus declares, "This is my body, which is given for you" (22:19). Luke's audience has expected this declaration from the beginning. Jesus's sacrifice, too, is qualitatively different from an animal sacrifice. Only a perfect human can assuage God's wrath. Jesus's identity as the Passover lamb in 2:22–24 also anticipates Simeon's famous last words in the following section (2:25–35), where he explicitly identifies Jesus as the long-awaited Isaianic servant.

"A Light for the Nations"

Luke records two interactions in 2:22–40 that are not documented in the other Gospels. The first interaction reinforces and develops our investigation (2:25–35). At the temple, Jesus's parents cross paths with a man named Simeon, an individual "waiting for the consolation of Israel" (2:25). "Consolation" (*paraklēsis*) here is an eschatological term that relates to Israel's restoration in the new creation (see the use of the cognate verb *parakaleō* in LXX Isa. 40:1; 49:13; 61:2). Like Elizabeth, Simeon is also filled with the Holy Spirit when he prophesies over baby Jesus (Luke 2:25).

Simeon's hymn drips with language from the book of Isaiah. Nearly every line alludes to Isaiah's message (see 2:30, quoting Isa. 40:5; 52:10), but I will focus on the last two lines:

> [Jesus will be] a light for revelation to the Gentiles,
>   and for glory to your people Israel. (Luke 2:32)[1]

At the end of the hymn, Simeon recalls a smattering of prominent servant passages in Isaiah where God's faithful servant will restore a remnant of Israelites and bring salvation to the nations. Foremost among these is Isaiah 49:6. According to Isaiah 49:3, the prophet labels Israel as "my [Yahweh's] servant."[2] And in the same breath, Isaiah predicts that the servant will

> raise up the tribes of Jacob
> and . . . bring back the preserved of Israel;
> I will make you as a light for the nations,
>   that my salvation may reach to the end of the earth. (Isa. 49:6)

---

1 James R. Edwards keenly observes, "It was rare in any genre of ancient literature to see Gentiles and Jews placed in positive opposition to one another, and rarer still to see Gentiles mentioned *before* Israel" (italics original; *The Gospel according to Luke*, PNTC [Grand Rapids, MI: Eerdmans, 2015], 86). If Luke is intentional about the order, then its significance is that Gentiles and Jews stand on equal ground. Both groups are in dire need of the servant's salvific ministry, and both will equally benefit.

2 Matthew S. Harmon suggests that the servant's ministry in Isa. 49 resembles Adam's vocation in the garden and "like Adam, the servant is formed by Yahweh (Isa. 49:5)" (*The Servant of the Lord and His Servant People: Tracing a Biblical Theme through the Canon*, NSBT 54 [Downers Grove, IL: IVP Academic, 2020], 124).

The servant must be an individual because he serves as the catalyst for the restoration of the remnant of Israelites or the "preserved of Israel."

The famous servant is the subject of four songs in the book of Isaiah: 42:1–9; 49:1–6; 50:4–9; and 52:13–53:12.[3] Yahweh promises to redeem captive Israel and plant them in the new creation *through* the servant's faithful and atoning ministry. The word "servant" (Heb. *'ebed*; Gk. *pais/doulos*) occurs nearly twenty times in Isaiah 40–66 and often refers to the idolatrous nation of Israel, who repeatedly disobeys God and fails to bring salvation to the nations. But within this same section of Isaiah, a righteous servant comes on the scene who obeys God, suffers on behalf of the covenant community, stimulates belief within the nations, and brings Israel out of exile (Isa. 42:1–9; 49:1–13; 50:4–11; 52:13–53:12). Following the servant's faithful obedience, Isaiah 55–66 switches to the plural "servants" (Heb. *'abadim*; Gk. *douloi*) to describe a righteous remnant of Israelites and Gentiles that fully identify with the one faithful servant (Isa. 56:6; 63:17; 65:8–9, 13–15; 66:14).[4] To summarize, Isaiah's faithful servant is an individual who is the pristine people of God, true Israel.[5] This faithful servant stimulates faith among unbelieving Israelites and forges a remnant within the nation. But that is not all. The servant will also bring the nations into the covenant community. The one servant will create a community of servants.

While Simeon and Mary are indeed servants (Luke 1:38; 2:29), Jesus is the ultimate servant of all. Admittedly, while Luke doesn't quite underscore Jesus's identity as the *suffering* servant of Isaiah like the other Evangelists, he still associates Jesus's death with the fourth Servant Song (see 22:37, quoting Isa. 53:12). Luke, though, is quick to

---

3   This paragraph excerpted and adapted from page 364 of *Handbook on the Gospels* by Benjamin L. Gladd, copyright © 2021. Used by permission of Baker Academic, a division of Baker Publishing Group.

4   See Daniel J. Brendsel, *"Isaiah Saw His Glory": The Use of Isaiah 52–53 in John 12*, BZNW 208 (Berlin: de Gruyter, 2014), 56–60.

5   Isaiah, like other Old Testament prophets, only expects the restoration of a remnant of Israelites (see 10:20–22; 11:11, 16; 28:5; 37:31–32; 46:3).

highlight Jesus's role as true Israel who forges a remnant within Israel that brings the gospel to the nations (see, e.g., Luke 3:6; Acts 1:8; 9:15; 13:47). Luke's appropriation of Isaiah 49:6 to Jesus is one of the closest passages in the New Testament that demonstrates Jesus's identity as true Israel. So Simeon's blessing on the child recognizes the initial fulfillment of these precious promises from the book of Isaiah and sets the trajectory of what will unfold in all of Luke-Acts.

Gentiles in Luke's Narrative

Though tracing the contours of the restoration of the nations in the Third Gospel deserves considerable attention, I only have the space to gain merely an appreciation of it. Gentile salvation, too, is a subset of Luke's larger program of highlighting the deliverance of all those who find themselves on society's margins—the poor, outcasts, prostitutes, children, women, and so on. Furthermore, Jesus's mission to the nations doesn't reach full bloom until the apostle Paul's ministry in the book of Acts. The good news begins in the little, insignificant town of Bethlehem in Judea (Luke 2:4) and reaches the heart of the Roman Empire (Acts 28:11–31).

An early sign that the nations take on special significance in the narrative is the extended Isaiah 40 quotation in Luke 3:4–6. All four Gospels quote Isaiah 40:3 and pair it with John the Baptist's ministry (Matt. 3:3; Mark 1:3; Luke 3:4–6; John 1:23), but only Luke cites the extended version of Isaiah 40:3–5. The last line of the quotation is worth exploring:

As it is written in the book of the words of Isaiah the prophet,

"The voice of one crying in the wilderness:
'Prepare the way of the Lord,
    make his paths straight.
Every valley shall be filled,
    and every mountain and hill shall be made low,
and the crooked shall become straight,

and the rough places shall become level ways,
and all flesh shall see the salvation of God.'" (Luke 3:4–6)

In the final line of the quotation, Luke follows the LXX.[6] The MT
reads, "All flesh shall see it [the glory of the Lord] together," whereas
the LXX reads, "all flesh shall see *the salvation* [*sōtērion*] of God"
(NETS). Though Luke may have lavishly followed the LXX and the
inclusion of "salvation" is merely happenstance, a far more likely sce-
nario is that Luke carefully preserved the LXX's rendering so that the
theme of "salvation" would surface. Cognates of "salvation" (*sōtērion*),
such as "savior" or "deliverance," are replete throughout Luke-Acts,
particularly as they relate to the Gentiles.[7] At the end of Acts, too,
Paul's final words are as follows: "let it be known to you [the Jewish
leaders] that this *salvation* [*sōtērion*] of God has been sent to the
Gentiles; they will listen" (Acts 28:28). Luke opens his project with a
prophecy that the nations would experience the long-awaited second
exodus, and at the end of Acts the apostle Paul claims—in Rome
nonetheless—that the gospel has indeed reached the Gentiles.

Armed with a better understanding of Luke's intention to include
Gentiles into the people of God, I will now sample a few passages that
demonstrate this reality. In Luke 4, immediately following the wilderness temptation, Jesus experiences rejection in Nazareth at the hands
of his own people (4:14–30; see discussion in chapter 7). During the
encounter, he explicitly aligns his ministry with two famed prophets—
Elijah and Elisha (4:24–27). Jesus isolates two events in their respective
ministries: the widow's willingness to feed Elijah despite the lack of food
for herself and her son (1 Kings 17:7–16) and Naaman's obedience to
Elisha by washing in the Jordan River to cleanse himself from leprosy
(2 Kings 5:1–14). Two Gentiles respond well to the prophets' summons,
whereas, in stark contrast, the Israelites are riddled with idolatry and
antagonism toward Elijah and Elisha. In isolating these two prophets,

---

6 One odd detail of Luke's quotation of Isa. 40:3–5 is his omission of 40:5a: "and the glory
   of the LORD shall be revealed."

7 See, e.g., Luke 7:3; 8:36; 17:19; 19:10; Acts 13:47; 15:11; 16:30–31; 27:43–44.

Jesus impugns the character of the Nazarenes and accuses them of rejecting the Lord's anointed.

Later, Luke once again invokes the narratives of Elijah and Elisha when Jesus raises a widow's son (Luke 7:11–17), an event that is unique to the Third Gospel. The LXX and Luke's narrative are quite similar (see table 3.1).

Table 3.1   Comparison of Elijah, Elisha, and Jesus Raising a Dead Son

Elijah	Elisha	Jesus
Elijah meets a woman at the "gate of the city" [LXX: *ton pylōna tēs poleōs*] (1 Kings / 3 Reigns 17:10)		Jesus meets a woman at the "gate of the town" [*tē pylē tēs poleōs*] (Luke 7:12)
The woman is a "widow" [LXX: *chēra*] (1 Kings / 3 Reigns 17:10)	The woman is married (2 Kings / 4 Reigns 4:9)	The woman is a "widow" [*chēra*] (Luke 7:12)
Son dies (1 Kings 17:17)	Son dies (2 Kings / 4 Reigns 4:20)	Son is dead (Luke 7:12)
Elijah "delivered [the son] to his mother" [LXX: *edōken auton tē mētri autou*] (1 Kings / 3 Reigns 17:23)	Elisha commands the Shunammite woman to "pick up your son" (2 Kings / 4 Reigns 4:36)	Jesus "gave [the son] to his mother" [*edōken auton tē mētri autou*] (Luke 7:15)
The woman recognizes that Elijah is indeed a "man of God" (1 Kings / 3 Reigns 17:24)	Shunammite woman "fell at [Elisha's] feet and did obeisance" (2 Kings / 4 Reigns 4:37 NETS)	The crowd recognizes that Jesus is a "prophet" (Luke 7:16)

Why does Luke continue to draw parallels between Jesus and Elijah/ Elisha? Because what was true in their day is true in Jesus's day. Jesus's own people reject him, whereas foreigners are quick to attach themselves to him. Several other examples of Gentiles coming to faith follow in Luke's narrative (see 8:26–39; 11:29–32). But, certainly, the most riveting example of Gentile salvation is the centurion at the crucifixion in 23:44–47.

All three Synoptics record the conversion of the centurion at the cross, underscoring its importance to all three narratives. The centurion, probably a Gentile, was in charge of carrying out Pilate's decree to crucify Jesus. The three Synoptics, too, detail the centurion's reaction to the events surrounding the crucifixion. In Luke's account, when the centurion observes the death of Jesus, he confesses, "Certainly this man was innocent!" (23:47), whereas Matthew and Mark record the centurion announcing, "Truly this was the Son of God" (Matt. 27:54; Mark 15:39 has "this man").

Luke's version, given the immediate context, is ironic on multiple levels. For example, earlier in the chapter, the Jewish leaders falsely accuse Jesus of "misleading" the Jewish people (Luke 23:2) and of being one who "stirs up the people" (23:5). Jesus is, of course, innocent of these accusations. The majority of the covenant community, the Jewish people, rejected the very one they were expecting. The centurion, a pagan and one who carried out the directives of the Roman officials, possessed more insight into Jesus's identity than the Jewish leaders. The Jewish people even possessed the Old Testament—the very Scriptures that predicted Jesus's death! This soldier may never have read or heard of the Old Testament. The point is that the centurion rightly declares Jesus to be innocent, but the religious leaders remain recalcitrant toward his identity. Luke also records that the centurion "praised God" (23:47). The same reaction echoes throughout the Third Gospel when individuals experience miracles or extraordinary events (see 2:20; 4:15; 5:25–26; 7:16; 13:13; 17:15; 18:43), revealing that God is truly at work. So when the centurion reacts in effusive praise, he sees beyond the externals of the cross and understands it for what it is—God's unrivaled wisdom and redemption manifested in Jesus (see 1 Cor. 1:18).

Consider the comfort the centurion's confession brings to Luke's Gentile audience. If God can forgive the centurion for executing his Son, then God can forgive Gentiles for all forms of rebellion. One's allegiance to Israel or possession of the Torah is not what ultimately matters but rather one's relationship to Christ. The same line of thinking carries over to ethnic Jews too. Immediately before Jesus's death, Luke famously includes a conversation between Jesus and one of the seditionists crucified with him. The criminal, probably a Jew,[8] acknowledges his guilt before God yet affirms Jesus's innocence (Luke 23:41). Jesus then promises the criminal that he will soon join him "in paradise" (23:43). Luke holds out two individuals, the Gentile centurion and the Jewish seditionist, as supreme examples of those who receive forgiveness on account of their trust in Christ.

The Relationship of Jews and Gentiles to Jesus as the True Israel of God

A major consequence of Jesus's identity as true Israel is the reconfiguring or reconstitution of God's people. In the old covenant, God generally related to his people through the administration of the Mosaic covenant, whereas in the new covenant, he relates to his people through his Son. Both groups, Jews and Gentiles, stand on equal footing through the person of Christ. This is precisely what Paul has in mind in Ephesians 3:6: "This *mystery* is that the Gentiles are fellow heirs, members of the same body, and partakers of the promise *in Christ Jesus* through the gospel." *Mystery*, found some twenty-eight times in the New Testament, is a crucial component of the New Testament and lies at the heart of how the New Testament relates to the Old. We can define "mystery" as the revelation of divine wisdom, the disclosure of knowledge that was largely hidden in the Old Testament but has been subsequently revealed in the New Testament.[9] Paul picks up on this revelatory framework and employs the term *mystery* in Ephesians 3 at a critical juncture.

Paul claims that Gentiles, together with Jewish believers, become true Israelites through faith in Christ, the embodiment of true Israel,

---

8   Eckhard J. Schnabel, *Jesus in Jerusalem: The Last Days* (Grand Rapids, MI: Eerdmans, 2018), 101.

9   See e.g., Dan. 2:20–23; Mark 4:11 and parallels; 1 Cor. 2:7; Col. 1:26; 1 Tim. 3:16. For further discussion of "mystery" in the Bible, see Benjamin L. Gladd, *Revealing the Mysterion: The Use of Mystery in Daniel and Second Temple Judaism with Its Bearing on First Corinthians*, BZNW 160 (Berlin: Walter de Gruyter, 2008); G. K. Beale and Benjamin L. Gladd, *Hidden but Now Revealed: A Biblical Theology of Mystery* (Downers Grove, IL: IVP Academic, 2014).

without having to identify themselves with some of the various nationalistic requirements under the Mosaic administration. Simply put, the "mystery" in Ephesians 3 entails *how* Gentiles become true Israelites in the new age. Whereas the Old Testament expected Gentiles to identify themselves with the Israelites externally, Paul argues that Gentiles mysteriously participate in the true Israel of God by faith alone in Christ. It was generally hidden in the Old Testament that Gentiles would join true Israel through faith alone.[10] *Since Christ is true Israel, all those who identify with him become true Israel.* This principle explains why Gentiles in Luke-Acts enjoy full access to the covenant community apart from the external requirements of the Mosaic law. God considers them to be true Israel because they trust in and follow Jesus, the long-awaited servant of Isaiah. Because this principle was largely hidden in the Old Testament, Peter is initially resistant to consuming unclean animals and to fellowshiping with Gentiles in Acts 10:1–33.[11] On account of Christ's work, all those who join themselves to Jesus are now acceptable to God and are deemed "clean." God admits the Gentiles into his Israelite family through their faith in Jesus and not by externally identifying themselves with the covenant community.

Jewish Priority and Jewish Unbelief

If Jews and Gentiles participate equally in the covenant community, in the words of Paul, "then what advantage has the Jew?" (Rom. 3:1). The answer is that God graciously and sovereignly chose the Israelites from the nations to be his covenant community, to reveal himself in a profound and unique way, and to relate to them in the form of a covenant. Romans 1:16, perhaps one of the most succinct statements

---

10 There are a handful of texts in the Old Testament that seem to indicate Gentiles will join the covenant community *without* adhering to external covenant markers. For example, according to Gen. 15:6, God justifies Abraham *before* his circumcision. This event anticipates the Gentiles participating in the covenant community without receiving the rite of circumcision (see Rom. 4:1–5, 9–17). See discussion in Beale and Gladd, *Hidden but Now Revealed*, 169–73.

11 On the other side of the coin, it could also be considered a "mystery" that Jews would not be required to adhere to the external particulars of the covenant in the new age.

concerning the interplay between Jews and Gentiles, states, "The gospel
. . . is the power of God that brings salvation to everyone who believes:
first to the Jew, then to the Gentile" (NIV; see also Rom. 9–11). Since
the patriarchs, the pattern of salvation has always been Israel first and
then the nations. God selects the nation of Israel *so that* the Israelites
may bring the nations into the covenant community (see Ex. 19:6).

Luke shows awareness of this pattern at various points throughout
his narrative. For example, Jesus's public ministry in Luke 4:14–8:21
takes place in Jewish territory. Then, when Jesus and the disciples
cross the Sea of Galilee, they move into Gentile territory (8:22–26).
The same redemptive movement is also found in Luke 9–10, where
Jesus first commissions the twelve in 9:1–6 to herald the gospel to
Israel. Then Jesus commissions the seventy-two disciples in 10:1–7, a
group representing a renewed humanity (note the symbolic allusion
to Gen. 10–11; see discussion in chapter 2). The seventy-two, though
their ministry is likely confined to Palestine, symbolize the gospel
reaching the nations. Acts 1:8 explicitly states that the apostles will be
Jesus's "witnesses in Jerusalem, and in all Judea and Samaria, and to
the end of the earth." Notice the geographic progression: "in all Judea
. . . to the end of the earth." Clearly, then, though Jews and Gentiles
participate fully in the true Israel of God, Jesus maintains the pattern
of Israel first and then the nations.

There is one more layer worth pursuing: the symbiotic relationship
between Jews and Gentiles in the Third Gospel. While Jews receive
the priority of salvation over Gentiles, Luke ironically connects Jewish
unbelief to Gentile belief. At points throughout the narrative, the Jewish
refusal of the gospel is the catalyst of Gentile acceptance of it. Above
we observed how Jesus's own community in Nazareth rejected him.
James Edwards captures the thrust of Luke 4: "The inaugural sermon in
Nazareth sets forth major theological and missional themes contained
in Luke-Acts, and the rejection of Jesus at Nazareth . . . in the [Third]
Gospel sets the stage for Paul's rejection on the same grounds in Acts."[12]

---

12 Edwards, *Gospel according to Luke*, 133.

Like Elijah and Elisha, Jesus will find more success among the nations (4:14–30). Nazareth, then, functions as a microcosm of the ministry of Jesus and the apostles.

We've now arrived at a theological conundrum. If the Old Testament anticipates *every* aspect of Jesus's ministry (see 1:1; 24:27, 44), then why do most Jews reject the very one they are expecting? The redemptive-historical framework of "mystery" is helpful in answering this question.

> In a very real sense, a complete or full meaning of large swaths of the Old Testament was partially and sometimes mostly "hidden" but now has been fully revealed, particularly as it relates to Christ. The incarnation of Christ, the embodiment of God's full revelation, sheds new light on the Old Testament, bringing about a fuller meaning of the prior revelation. . . . Full or complete meaning was "hidden" in the Old Testament but has now been "revealed" in light of Christ.[13]

The biblical conception of mystery, then, explains how Jesus's ministry can simultaneously fulfill Old Testament expectations yet remain concealed from those who witness it. The Nazarenes (and the remainder of Jewish unbelievers) fail to read the Old Testament rightly in accordance with Christ. Jesus doesn't fault the Nazarenes for the lack of access to the Scriptures. Indeed, many of them likely know a great deal of the Old Testament. The problem lies in their reluctance to connect Jesus to the heart of the Old Testament on the level of explicit prophecies and typological patterns.

Does the Old Testament anticipate such a rejection? All four Gospels answer in the affirmative and quote the same Old Testament passage when they do so. The four Evangelists quote from Isaiah 6 as judgment on those who reject Jesus's message (see Matt. 13:11–15 // Mark 4:10–12 // Luke 8:10; John 12:38–40; Acts 28:25–28). Matthew explicitly claims that rejecting Jesus fulfills Isaiah 6:9–10 (Matt. 13:14). The Gospel authors broadly apply Isaiah 6:9–10 to unbelievers within

---

13 Beale and Gladd, *Hidden but Now Revealed*, 292–93.

Israel, and Luke even targets the Jewish leaders at the end of Acts. Jesus himself quotes Isaiah 6:9–10 during his Galilean ministry in the Synoptics, whereas John quotes Isaiah 6:10 during his account of Passion Week. Paul quotes Isaiah 6:9–10 during his Roman imprisonment at the end of Acts. Clearly, then, Isaiah 6 provides some of the theological basis for the Jewish rejection of the Messiah.

According to Isaiah 6, Israel is corrupt to its very core. In Isaiah 6:9–10, Israel is blind and deaf like the idols they worship.[14] The nation of Israel in the first century, represented by the Jewish leaders, has rejected Jesus's message because they too have committed idolatry. The first-century religious leaders don't bow down to physical idols but worship Torah and oral tradition. Jesus gets to the heart of the matter in John 5:39–40: "You search the Scriptures because you think that in them you have eternal life; and it is they that bear witness about me, yet you refuse to come to me that you may have life." Jerry Ray rightly puts all the pieces together of Luke's complex portrayal of Gentile salvation and the fulfillment of Old Testament promises:

> The Jews reject their Messiah and refuse to believe the gospel of salvation. However, instead of undoing the divine will, they ironically bring about its very accomplishment. Their rejection of Jesus as Messiah leads to his death and resurrection, thereby fulfilling scriptural prophecies which define his messiahship. Their rejection of the church's gospel leads to the Gentile mission, resulting in the fulfillment of the biblical mandate to proclaim the messianic salvation to all nations. . . . The very thing that seeks to hinder the plan of God—the Jewish rejection of Jesus and the gospel—in actuality enables God's plan to be realized.[15]

To recap, Jesus first announces the presence of the kingdom to the Jewish people. But the majority of Israelites fail to trust in Jesus, and only

---

14 Cf. Deut. 29:3–4; Pss. 115:4–8; 135:15–18; Jer. 5:21; Ezek. 12:2.

15 Jerry Lynn Ray, *Narrative Irony in Luke-Acts: The Paradoxical Interaction of Prophetic Fulfillment and Jewish Rejection* (Lewiston, NY: Mellen Biblical, 1996), 132.

a few ethnic Jews from within the nation believe his message. Jewish rejection oddly precipitates the flourishing of the gospel among the nations.

Who Is Israel?[16]

Now that I've discussed Jesus's identity as true Israel and the Gentiles' full participation in the covenant community, I am in a better position to define what I mean by the general term *Israel*. Does it primarily denote an *ethnic* relationship between Abraham and his descendants? Or does it primarily refer to a spiritual status between God and his people? The name "Israel" first occurs following Jacob's wrestling with the angel in Genesis. The angel gives the patriarch that name because he had "striven with God and with men, and [had] prevailed" (Gen. 32:28). Even the name Israel probably means "God fights" or "God struggles." As many commentators argue, this event signals a new redemptive phase in Jacob's life. The name change demonstrates a fundamental shift in how Jacob relates to God. Hans LaRondelle explains, "The name 'Israel' from the beginning symbolizes a personal relation of reconciliation with God. The rest of Holy Scripture never loses sight of this sacred root of the name."[17]

Certainly, the Old Testament employs the term *Israel* to refer to a physical or ethnic dimension to the people of God, but the spiritual dimension remains paramount. To be part of Israel means to be part of the covenant community. The Old Testament is filled with examples of non-Israelites, or Gentiles, joining the covenant community and receiving an inheritance in the land. Their relationship to the covenant is determined ultimately by faith in God's promises.

Many examples could be given, but two will suffice. Psalm 87 speaks of Gentiles being "born in Zion" at the end of history and becoming indistinguishable from ethnic Israelites:

---

16 This section is taken and adapted from pages 52–54 of *From Adam and Israel to the Church* by Benjamin L. Gladd, ©2019 by Benjamin L. Gladd. Used by permission of InterVarsity Press. www.ivpress.com.

17 Hans K. LaRondelle, *The Israel of God in Prophecy: Principles of Prophetic Interpretation* (Berrien Springs, MI: Andrews University Press, 1983), 82.

The LORD loves the gates of Zion
more than all the other dwellings of Jacob.
Glorious things are said of you,
city of God:
"I will record Rahab and Babylon
among those who acknowledge me—
Philistia too, and Tyre, along with Cush—
and will say, 'This one was born in Zion.'"
Indeed, of Zion it will be said,
"This one and that one were born in her,
and the Most High himself will establish her."
The LORD will write in the register of the peoples:
"This one was born in Zion." (Ps. 87:2–6 NIV)

The psalmist predicts that some of Israel's neighbors—Egypt, Babylon, Philistia, Tyre, and Cush—will be considered full-blown citizens of the covenant community at the end of history. Both native Israelites and Gentiles will bear the honorable title "born in Zion." That is, Gentiles will one day be called "Israel." The point is that the term *Israel* is not ultimately ethnic in nature but spiritual.

The second example is found in Isaiah 19, where the prophet anticipates the restoration of the nations at the end of history. According to Isaiah, the Lord says, "Blessed be Egypt my people, and Assyria the work of my hands, and Israel my inheritance" (Isa. 19:25). Throughout the Old Testament, Israel is often described as being God's "people" (Ps. 100:3), "the work of [his] hands" (Isa. 29:23; 64:8), and his "inheritance/ heritage" (Deut. 4:20; 9:26; 32:9; Ps. 78:71). In a striking manner, Isaiah applies such language to Egypt and Assyria! God considers the remnant within all three nations—Egypt, Assyria, and Israel—to be part of his covenant community (Isa. 19:24).

What does this discussion of the nature of Israel have to do with Luke's portrayal of Jews and Gentiles? The Jewish people are externally distinguished from the nations in their adherence to the covenant. The faithful remnant within the Jewish people is not only externally distinguished from the pagan nations but also spiritually separated. Jewish believers trust the veritable promises of God, and their adherence to the law flows from a heart of faith. This explains why the apostle Paul distinguishes between those who are Jews "outwardly" and "inwardly" (Rom. 2:28–29). To put the matter bluntly, "not all who are born into the nation of Israel are truly members of God's people!" (Rom. 9:6 NLT). At various points throughout Luke-Acts, Jewish believers stand in stark contrast to Jewish unbelievers. Jewish unbelievers externally identify with Israel's law through circumcision, worship at the temple, Sabbath observance, and so on; yet their participation within the covenant community is only skin deep. Their bodies may be circumcised, but their hearts are not.

The matter is a bit more complex with Gentiles, however. Gentiles are naturally and externally excluded from God's covenant with Israel. How do Gentiles participate in this covenant? According to the Old Testament, they become members of the covenant, like Jewish believers, by trusting in God's promises of deliverance. As a result of placing their faith in God, these Gentiles also take on the requirements of the law of Moses. So when Gentiles desired to join the covenant community before the coming of Christ, they generally attended the synagogue, obeyed Sabbath regulations, followed dietary restrictions, and so on (e.g., Cornelius).[18] The Old Testament prophetic literature even generally anticipated that the nations would become nearly indistinguishable from Israelites at the end of history by externally identifying themselves, at least to some degree, with Israel (e.g., Isa. 56:3–8; 66:18–21; Zech. 14:16–19). But on account of Christ's work, the nations can "mysteriously" join the true Israel by trusting in and identifying with him. This unique redemptive-historical twist opened the door for the gospel to flourish among the Gentiles within the larger Roman Empire.

By Faith

Our final brief discussion on the theme of faith gets at the heart of Jewish and Gentile participation in the true people of God. Early in

---

18 There were degrees of Jewish proselytism, of course, since most "God-fearing" Gentiles sympathetic to Judaism objected to the Jewish rite of circumcision.

his ministry, Jesus, perceiving the faith of the men lowering the para-lyzed man through the roof, announces, "Man, your sins are forgiven you" (Luke 5:20). The declaration prompts the Jewish leaders to take umbrage at Jesus's actions, because "who can forgive sins but God alone?" (5:21). Then, in one of the most riveting declarations in all of Luke's Gospel, Jesus claims that he "has authority on earth to forgive sins" (5:24). The connection between faith and forgiveness of sins is apparent. The remission of sins is therefore bound up with faith in Jesus, not in the sacrificial system of the temple. Two chapters later, Jesus commends the faith of the God-fearing centurion: "I tell you [the crowd], not even in Israel have I found such faith" (7:9; cf. 8:25). Then, a "woman of the city, who was a sinner," anoints Jesus's feet with expensive oil (7:37), prompting Jesus to declare that her sins are forgiven because her faith has saved her (7:48, 50). These outsiders stand in contrast to those within Israel, even the disciples at times (see 8:25; 12:28; 18:9), who have had the privilege of learning about God in the Old Testa-ment yet refuse to embrace the Son of Man (9:41; 12:46; 16:31). Faith in Jesus, not in one's ethnicity or social standing, is the means by which an individual stands before a holy God and subsequently joins the true covenant community—that is, true Israel.

The faith of the disciples in Luke's Gospel is also worth mentioning. As the narrative progresses, so does their faith. In the stilling of the storm, the disciples are still trying to piece together Jesus's identity as Israel's Messiah and her divine Lord. Jesus's piercing question, "Where is your faith?" jolts Luke's readers (8:25). But as Jesus continues to reveal himself in word and deed, the faith of the disciples slowly but steadily grows (see 9:18–20). The disciples respond with a desire for Jesus to increase their faith (17:5); they want bigger faith. But more is not always better. It is the *quality* of the faith that counts. They must place their faith squarely in Jesus. A little faith, the size of a mustard seed, has great power—enough to uproot and plant a mulberry tree (17:6). Several chapters earlier, Jesus compares the growth of the kingdom to that of a mustard seed that, though incredibly small, becomes a powerful tree (13:19; cf. Ezek. 17:23; Dan. 4:20–22). The kingdom, too, begins with a single person, Jesus, but eventually expands to the end of the earth (Acts 1:8). The disciples must possess genuine faith in the advancement of the kingdom that is rooted in Jesus. At the end of the narrative, we finally see the disciples fully placing their faith in Jesus because they have believed the witness of the Old Testament (Luke 24:25–27, 44–49). Faith in Christ flows from a faith in Israel's Scriptures.

Conclusion

Simeon's assertion that Jesus will be "a light for revelation to the Gentiles, / and for glory to your people Israel" (Luke 2:32) is a central tenet of Luke-Acts. The first line, "a light for revelation to the Gentiles," alludes to the prophecy of Isaiah 49:6. By applying this prophecy to Jesus, Simeon perceives Jesus's identity to be the long-awaited faithful servant of Israel. Jesus is true Israel who restores a remnant of Israelites but who also brings salvation to the nations.

Today, most Christians, particularly in the West, often struggle with reading the Bible and seeing themselves as participants in its grand story line. Though two thousand years separate us from the New Testament, we must resist the temptation to read the Bible as mere observers. The story of the Bible, spanning Genesis 1–2 to Revelation 21–22, is *our* story. Christ is the true people of God, and all those who unswervingly trust in the Son of Man likewise inherit his identity. There are no second-class citizens in the kingdom.

4

The Way of Life

GOD'S PROMISE TO DELIVER HIS PEOPLE in a second exodus prominently runs throughout the Old Testament. The first act of redemption prophetically anticipates a second, final act of redemption. The term *exodus* includes all the events from Israel's deliverance from Egyptian bondage to Israel's entrance into the promised land. It entails some forty years of God's acts of redemption and testing. The first exodus becomes a prophetic blueprint—a framework—of a future, eschatological second exodus.

All four Gospels and the New Testament at large tap into this prophetic theme and relate it to Christ's life, death, and resurrection. Luke's Gospel and the book of Acts are particularly sensitive to the second exodus. We can discern Luke's awareness of it not only in his retelling of individual episodes during Jesus's ministry but also in his larger structural outline of his narrative. The aim of this chapter is to discuss the Old Testament anticipation of the second exodus and then demonstrate its fulfillment in Luke's Gospel. While there are several exodus themes embedded within Luke's narrative (e.g., the stilling of the storm, the Passover meal, and the suffering servant), the focus here is to appreciate the Third Gospel's emphasis on the *journey* to the promised land of the new creation.

The Old Testament Expectation of the Second Exodus

The Old Testament extensively anticipates a second exodus. Five of the first six books of the Old Testament largely take place during the exodus (Exodus, Leviticus, Numbers, Deuteronomy, and Joshua). All the material from Exodus 19:1 to Numbers 10:10 takes place at Sinai. The remaining portions of the Old Testament either presuppose a robust knowledge of the exodus or address it in one form or another.

The Exodus in the Pentateuch and in Joshua

R. E. Watts argues that the exodus entails "three fundamental elements: Israel's deliverance from Egypt; the journey through the wilderness; and the arrival in the Promised Land."[1] Watts then helpfully distills eleven motifs contained within the exodus:[2]

1. The patriarchal promise of offspring (Ex. 1:1–20)
2. The revelation of the divine name (Ex. 3:1–4:17)
3. The hardening of Pharaoh's heart (Ex. 4:21; 7:3; 8:15, 32; 9:12; 10:1)
4. Signs and wonders (Ex. 7:1–12:32)
5. The Passover and the firstborn (Ex. 12:1–32)
6. Crossing the sea (Ex. 14:1–31)
7. Journey to the mountain of God (Ex. 15:22–19:1)
8. Giving of the law and instructions concerning the tabernacle (Ex. 19:1–40:38; Lev. 1:1–27:34)
9. The golden calf (Ex. 32:1–35)
10. Israel in the wilderness (Num. 10:11–Deut. 34:12)
11. Arrival in the promised land (Josh. 3:1–24:33)

While other themes could be mentioned, these eleven are sufficient in giving us a foundation for discussing the exodus.

Israel's deliverance from Egypt and arrival in the promised land are not without anticipation. Some scholars rightly argue that the exodus

---

1 R. E. Watts, "Exodus," in *New Dictionary of Biblical Theology*, ed. T. D. Alexander and B. S. Rosner (Downers Grove, IL: InterVarsity Press, 2000), 479.
2 Watts, "Exodus," 479–82. Watts, though, lists "a new era" as the eleventh item and then describes it as Israel's new birth. Therefore, for his eleventh item, I substituted Israel's arrival in the promised land. Also, Watts strangely omits the giving of the law, so I added that to the eighth motif.

must be connected to the whole of Genesis, especially Genesis 1–3.[3] For example, several connections exist between the ten plagues (Ex. 7:1–12:32) and the creation account in Genesis 1–2. The movement runs from de-creation to new creation. Pharaoh, too, can be compared to the serpent in Genesis 3, as both characters are marshalled against God's people. According to Exodus 4:22, God calls Israel his "firstborn son," a phrase that recalls Adam being created in God's "image" and "likeness" (Gen 1:26–28; cf. 5:1). The terms "likeness" and "image" are then used to describe Seth, who is Adam's "son" (Gen. 5:3). The point, then, is that the presence of these terms in Genesis 1 and 5 implies that Adam is God's son. Just as God fathers Adam, he also fathers Israel. We could draw many more lines of continuity between Adam and Israel, but the point is clear enough: God's creation/redemption of Israel in the exodus mirrors his creation of Adam and Eve in the garden.

Sadly, at the end of Deuteronomy, Moses predicts that God will, on account of Israel's idolatry, "scatter [the Israelites] among all peoples, from one end of the earth to the other" (Deut. 28:64). Then, remarkably, Moses claims that God will "bring [them] back in ships to Egypt" (Deut. 28:68; cf. 28:26–28; 29:26–28). The exodus, God's redemption of his people from Egyptian bondage, will be reversed. Israel will find itself back in figurative Egypt. This prediction came true several hundred years later when Assyria exiled Israel in the eighth century BC and Babylon exiled the nation in the sixth century BC (see 2 Kings 17; 23). Something must be done so that the cycle of idolatry and exile will be broken.

Prophetic Expectations of a New Exodus

Throughout the Old Testament, especially in the Prophets, God promised to deliver Israel out of bondage at the end of history and bring

---

3   See, for example, Stephen G. Dempster, *Dominion and Dynasty: A Theology of the Hebrew Bible*, NSBT 18 (Downers Grove, IL: InterVarsity Press, 2003), 93–107; Meredith G. Kline, *Kingdom Prologue: Genesis Foundations for a Covenantal Worldview* (Eugene, OR: Wipf & Stock, 2006), 30; Benjamin L. Gladd, *From Adam and Israel to the Church: A Biblical Theology of the People of God*, ESBT 1 (Downers Grove, IL: IVP Academic, 2019), 35–56.

them to the promised land (e.g., Jer. 31:7–11, 31–34; Hos. 11:10–11; Mic. 5:3). The book of Isaiah, more than any other Old Testament book, portrays the restoration of Israel from Babylon as a second exodus. Describing Israel's return to the promised land, Isaiah 43 uses language from Israel's first exodus:

> When you pass through the waters, I will be with you.
> . . . .
> I give Egypt as your ransom.
> . . . .
> Thus says the LORD,
>   who makes a way in the sea,
>   a path in the mighty waters,
> who brings forth chariot and horse,
>   army and warrior;
> they lie down, they cannot rise,
>   they are extinguished, quenched like a wick.
> . . . .
> Behold, I am doing a new thing;
>   now it springs forth, do you not perceive it?
> I will make a way in the wilderness
>   and rivers in the desert. (Isa. 43:2, 3, 16–17, 19)

Isaiah predicts that Israel will once again "pass through the waters" (Isa. 43:2), a clear reference to Israel's march through the Red Sea (Ex. 14). Connections between the first and second exodus are not confined to Isaiah 43. Elsewhere Isaiah says that the Lord will manifest his glory (Isa. 40:5; cf. Ex. 16:7, 10; 24:16) and repeat the mountaintop experience at Sinai (Isa. 64:1–3; cf. Ex. 19). Yahweh promises to guide Israel through the wilderness as he originally did in a cloud, both in front and at the rear of the caravan:

> For you shall not go out in haste,
>   and you shall not go in flight;

for the Lord will go before you,

and the God of Israel will be your rear guard. (Isa. 52:12;

cf. 40:11; Ex. 13:21–22)

As the Lord provided food and water in the first exodus, so too in the second:

They shall feed along the ways;

on all bare heights shall be their pasture;

they shall not hunger or thirst,

neither scorching wind nor sun shall strike them,

for he who has pity on them will lead them,

and by springs of water will guide them. (Isa. 49:9b–10; cf.

Num. 10:11–32:42)

The famous servant of Isaiah will be instrumental in delivering Israel from Babylonian captivity (Isa. 42:1–9; 49:1–6; 50:4–9; 52:13–53:12).

One major difference remains between the first exodus and the second: the Old Testament expects the second exodus to be a final, consummate event. This explains why Isaiah interprets Israel's arrival in the promised land as an entrance into the new creation. For example,

For behold, I create new heavens

and a new earth,

and the former things shall not be remembered

or come into mind. (Isa. 65:17)

The "former things" likely refers to God's dealings with Israel in the first exodus (see Isa. 42:9; 43:9, 18; 46:9; 48:3). Isaiah views the totality of Israel's history as God redeeming his people. Notice, too, that Old Testament prophets do not anticipate a third exodus. In other words, Israel's history is bookended with two exoduses. In the first exodus, God redeems his people from Egyptian bondage and carries them into the promised land. In the second exodus, at the end of history, God will once again redeem his people and plant them in the new creation.

Fulfillment of the Second Exodus in Luke

One striking difference between the Synoptics and the Gospel of John is Jesus's journey to Jerusalem. John's Gospel presents Jesus journeying multiple times to Jerusalem to celebrate various feasts (John 2:13, 23; 5:1; 6:4; 7:2; 10:22; 11:55; 12:1; 13:1), whereas the Synoptics present a single journey to Jerusalem. Luke, like Matthew and Mark, traces Jesus's public ministry from the wilderness in Judea to Galilee, where he spends the bulk of his career. Then, at the end of his career, he turns south to Jerusalem where he will suffer, die, and be raised to life. All three Synoptics record Jesus's journey from Galilee to Jerusalem, but Luke devotes more than *one-third* of his narrative to the journey (Matt. 19:1–20:34; Mark 8:22–10:52; Luke 9:51–19:27). Luke also records a unique second journey—the famous journey from Jerusalem to Emmaus (Luke 24:13–35). These two journeys represent more than geographic information though. Luke intends his readers to view them along redemptive-historical lines, a movement from Egypt to the promised land, from darkness to light, from bondage to freedom, and from ignorance to enlightenment.[4]

Luke sets the trajectory of this key dimension of Jesus's career with John the Baptist in 3:3–6:[5]

---

4   The movement into exile begins in Gen. 3:24, where God "drove out" Adam and "at the east of the garden of Eden he placed the cherubim and a flaming sword." From Gen. 3 onward, eastwardly movement often symbolizes a movement away from God's presence in Eden (see, e.g., Gen. 4:16; 13:11; 25:6). Assyria and Babylon—empires that lie to the east—embody exile. This is probably why the temple faces east and why the high priest travels west to enter the Most Holy Place on the Day of Atonement (see discussion in Michael Morales, *Who Shall Ascend the Mountain of the Lord? A Biblical Theology of the Book of Leviticus*, NSBT 37 [Leicester, UK: Apollos, 2015], 176–77). To travel west out of exile and toward the promised land is a return to Eden.

5   David W. Pao states that the Isa. 40:3–5 quotation in Luke 3:3–6 is one of "two lengthy quotations from Isaiah [that] provide an interpretative framework for the reading of this section as well as the entire Lukan writings" ("Luke, Book of" in *Dictionary of the New Testament Use of the Old Testament*, ed. G. K Beale, D. A. Carson, Benjamin L. Gladd, and Andrew D. Naselli [Grand Rapids, MI: Baker Academic], forthcoming).

And he went into all the region around the Jordan, proclaiming a baptism of repentance for the forgiveness of sins. As it is written in the book of the words of Isaiah the prophet,

> "The voice of one crying in the wilderness:
> 'Prepare the way of the Lord,
>   make his paths straight.
> Every valley shall be filled,
>   and every mountain and hill shall be made low,
> and the crooked shall become straight,
>   and the rough places shall become level ways,
> and all flesh shall see the salvation of God.'"

Luke quotes from Isaiah 40, one of the most important passages in the book of Isaiah and the entire Old Testament, which explains why the New Testament often recalls it (see, e.g., Matt. 3:3; Mark 1:3; Luke 1:76; John 1:23; Rev. 1:5; 18:6). Isaiah 40 announces the return of God's people who are enslaved in Babylon. Just as God led his people through the wilderness and into the promised land, he will lead the covenant community from Babylonian exile to the promised land. Therefore, when Luke quotes the eschatologically charged Isaiah 40:3–5, he claims that John the Baptist is proclaiming the end of Israel's spiritual exile and her long-awaited return (see Luke 1:76, 79).

Two observations are in order. First, although Luke only explicitly cites Isaiah 40:3–5, he has many other passages from Isaiah in mind, if not all of Isaiah 40–66. C. H. Dodd, several decades ago, made a critical observation about how New Testament authors draw from the Old Testament. He argued that the New Testament authors were aware of the broad contexts of their Old Testament quotations and do not focus merely on a single passage.[6] Explicit Old Testament quotations often function like the tip of an iceberg that readers perceive, but the New Testament author expects the readers to consider what lies beneath

---

6   C. H. Dodd, *According to the Scriptures: The Sub-Structure of New Testament Theology* (London: Nisbet, 1952), 126–27.

the tip—that is, the broad context of the explicit quotation. The use of Isaiah 40:3–5 in Luke 3:4–6 falls into this category. Though Luke only quotes a mere three verses of Isaiah 40, he invites his readers to consider the immediate and broad context of Isaiah 40–66. Isaiah 40:3–5 is, then, a signpost that summons Luke's audience to recall Isaiah's broad message of return from exile, the new creation, and the victory of the messianic servant figure. John the Baptist's role in heralding Isaiah's second exodus in Luke 3 makes good sense in light of the broad context of Isaiah 40–66. This explains why Luke often draws from the book of Isaiah in Luke-Acts (see discussion in the introduction).

Second, Brevard Childs makes a number of important comments on the significance of Isaiah 40:3–5. He rightly connects the imagery of the highway in Isaiah 40:3 to "the transformation of the wilderness into a garden . . . in order to facilitate the return of the exiles" (see Isa. 35:6-7; 41:18–19; 43:19).[7] Yet not only does he relate the highway to the theme of the new creation, but Childs also goes on to claim that the highway recalls Israel's "exodus from Egypt" and that the "two events [the transformation of the wilderness and the second exodus] are fused into a single all-encompassing paradigm of divine deliverance."[8] In other words, the highway in Isaiah 40:3–5 operates as a metonymy, a figure of speech that functions as a part for the whole.[9] *The path or highway represents the entire event of the second exodus.* Finally, Childs argues that "the strongest intertextual tie with 40:3–5 is found in chapter 35."[10] Isaiah 35 mentions the transformation of the wilderness into an Edenic environment (Isa. 35:1–2, 6b–7a), the presence of a "highway" or the "Way of Holiness" where only the ritually pure may travel (35:8), the reversal of physical maladies (Isa. 35:3, 5–6a), and,

---

7   Brevard S. Childs, *Isaiah*, OTL (Louisville: Westminster John Knox, 2001), 299.

8   Childs, *Isaiah*, 299.

9   The book of Isaiah variously describes this "path" as a "highway" (Heb. *mesillah* / Gk. *diodos*) for a remnant of Israelites (11:16; cf. 62:10), the "Way of Holiness" (Heb. *derek haqqōdesh* / Gk. *hodos hagia*) for pure Israelites (35:8), and a "highway" (Heb. *mesillah* / Gk. *hodos*) for Gentiles (19:23).

10   Childs, *Isaiah*, 299.

climactically, the "joy" of the redeemed as they experience the "glory of the Lord" (Isa. 35:2, 10).

If we connect Jesus's ministry to passages such as Isaiah 35 and 40, then many redemptive-historical chips fall into place in the Third Gospel. For example, Luke's narrative presents four broad movements of the wilderness/highway theme:

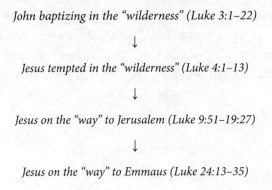

John baptizing in the "wilderness" (Luke 3:1–22)

↓

Jesus tempted in the "wilderness" (Luke 4:1–13)

↓

Jesus on the "way" to Jerusalem (Luke 9:51–19:27)

↓

Jesus on the "way" to Emmaus (Luke 24:13–35)

While commentators don't often relate Jesus's wilderness temptation to Isaiah's second exodus theme, a deep connection remains. Notice the pairing of "wilderness" and "way" in Luke 3:4–5: "The voice of one crying *in the wilderness* [*en tē erēmō*]: 'Prepare *the way* [*tēn hodon*] of the Lord.'"[11] Jesus's baptism in the Jordan River by John the Baptist (3:21–22) and his subsequent temptation in the "wilderness" (*erēmos*; 4:1–13) rehearse the first exodus when Israel wanders in the wilderness (see chapter 5). Jesus typologically repeats Israel's steps: Israel's unfaithfulness prophetically anticipates Jesus's faithfulness. As a result of his success, Jesus now liberates his people from spiritual exile in a second exodus. In other words, Jesus's own personal first exodus makes Israel's second exodus possible.

---

11 Isaiah often groups "wilderness" and "way" (see LXX Isa. 35:1, 2, 6, 8; 40:3; 41:18, 27; 43:16, 19, 20; 51:3, 10; 62:4, 10). Sometimes God transforms the "wilderness" into a "way" (e.g., Isa. 35), or he cuts a "way" *through* the "wilderness" (Isa. 43:19).

When Herod imprisons John the Baptist, John sends his disciples with a message for Jesus: "Are you the one who is to come, or shall we look for another?" (Luke 7:20). Jesus's response is somewhat surprising: "Go and tell John what you have seen and heard: the blind receive their sight, the lame walk, lepers are cleansed, and the deaf hear, the dead are raised up, the poor have good news preached to them" (7:22). Jesus draws from Isaiah 29:18 and 35:5–6. Isaiah 35, as I mentioned above, concerns the transformation of God's people on the road to the promised land in the second, future exodus. Jesus's miracles, then, should be partly viewed as Jesus preparing the covenant community for entrance into the new creation. Jesus restores not only individuals' souls but also their bodies. These miracles, too, are a foretaste of God's fully restoring believers' bodies for inhabiting the new earth at the end of history.

The Journey from Galilee to Jerusalem

Jesus's journey from Galilee to Jerusalem in Luke 9:51–19:27 should be understood as a decisive movement in the redemption of the covenant community. At the transfiguration, an event that immediately precedes Jesus's southward journey, Luke drops a significant clue on how his readers should view the next stage of Jesus's career in 9:51–19:27. When Jesus was transfigured on the mountain (9:28–29), "two men were talking with him, Moses and Elijah, who appeared in glory and spoke of his *departure* [*tēn exodon*], which he was about to accomplish at Jerusalem" (9:30–31). Matthew and Mark only mention that Moses and Elijah spoke to Jesus (Matt. 17:3; Mark 9:4), whereas Luke divulges *what* they discussed: the three conversed about Jesus's "departure" or *exodos* in Jerusalem.

The term *departure* is thick with layers of meaning. On the one hand, his departure certainly means his death—the transformation of an earthly body to a heavenly one.[12] But the term also contains overtones of a second exodus. Jesus's death and resurrection, his own personal

---

12 See, e.g., 2 Pet. 1:15; Philo, *Creation* 119.

exodus, are the climax of his redemptive act of delivering his people from the enslavement of sin and securing a place for them to dwell in the new creation.[13] The exodus of the covenant community is not simply a deliverance *from* sin and the devil. It also entails Jesus's leading his church *to* the new creational promised land.

In Acts 13:17–41, when Paul preaches in a synagogue in Antioch, he first recounts God's covenant with the patriarchs, Israel's exodus from Egypt, her wilderness wanderings, and the conquest (Acts 13:17–19). Then, he colorfully describes Jesus's arrival on the scene as a "coming" (*eisodos*): "Before his *coming* [*eisodou*], John had proclaimed a baptism of repentance to all the people of Israel" (Acts 13:24). The term "coming" does not refer to Jesus's incarnation but to his baptism (Luke 3:21–22). While not part of the Lukan corpus, Jesus's famous words in John 14:6 should be brought to bear in this discussion: "I am the *way* [*hodos*], and the truth, and the life. No one comes to the Father except through me." A few commentators explain that the reference to "way" here in John 14:6 recalls Old Testament texts such as Isaiah 40:3.[14]

Taking Luke 9:31, Acts 13:24, and John 14:6 together, significant portions of Jesus's career should be viewed through the lens of the long-awaited second exodus.[15] Perhaps I could tentatively claim that

---

13 The Greek term *exodos* is often used in Jewish literature as a reference to the exodus of Israel from Egypt (e.g., LXX Ex. 19:1; Num. 33:38; 1 Kings 6:1; Josephus, *Ant.* 2.271, 291, 309; Philo, *Migration* 15; *Moses* 1.105; T. Benj. 12.4). Scholars often argue that Luke's use of *exodos* in 9:31 is, in some way, tied to the theme of a second exodus. For example, John Nolland says, "There must also be an allusion here to the exodus of the people of Israel from Egypt under Moses' leadership" (*Luke 9:21–18:34*, WBC [Grand Rapids, MI: Zondervan, 1993], 499).

14 E.g., Andreas J. Köstenberger, "John," in *Commentary on the New Testament Use of the Old Testament*, ed. G. K. Beale and D. A. Carson (Grand Rapids, MI: Baker Academic, 2007), 489. See Craig S. Keener who argues that "way" in John 14:6 corresponds to the same idea in Acts 9:2; 18:25–26; 19:9, 23; 22:4; 24:14, 22 (*The Gospel of John: A Commentary*, 2 vols. [Grand Rapids, MI: Baker Academic, 2003], 2:942–43).

15 N. T. Wright famously argues that the second exodus and the end of the exile is *the* controlling framework for understanding Jesus's life, death, and resurrection (see especially N. T. Wright, *The New Testament and the People of God* [Minneapolis: Fortress, 1992]; N. T. Wright, *Jesus and the Victory of God* [Minneapolis: Press, 1996]). I remain unconvinced that all of Jesus's ministry should be filtered through this lens. My own view is that Jesus's ultimate concern is the redemption of his people from sin and guilt. Since

the time before Jesus's arrival could be considered a "pre-exodus" (Acts 13:24). During his ministry, he is the "way" to the promised land (John 14:6). After his death, resurrection, and ascension, he inaugurates the "exodus" (Luke 9:31) in a more decisive way. Regardless of how we assemble the mosaic, Luke clearly keeps his finger on the exodus theme throughout Luke-Acts.

Shortly after the transfiguration, Jesus turns south to Jerusalem. For nearly ten chapters (Luke 9:51–19:27), Jesus leads the disciples, slowly but surely, to Jerusalem. According to 3:3–6, John the Baptist's ministry is the catalyst of the end-time restoration of true Israel, the remnant, from Babylonian captivity. All four Gospels associate John with preparing the "way of *the Lord* [*kyrios*]" (Matt. 3:3; Mark 1:3–4; Luke 3:3–4; John 1:23). But who comes after John? Jesus himself! John the Baptist is the messenger, and Jesus is the "Lord"—Israel's God in the flesh. From the outset, the Gospels strikingly present Jesus as Yahweh incarnate, the Lord, who fulfills the promises he spoke to the prophet Isaiah hundreds of years earlier.[16]

If I am right to connect Jesus with the identity of Yahweh at the beginning of Luke's narrative, then Luke encourages his readers to view Jesus's journey from Galilee to Jerusalem through this same light. The term *hodos* (usually translated "way" or "road"), while spanning the Third Gospel, appears often in the journey to Jerusalem (Luke 9:57; 10:4, 31; 11:6; 12:58; 14:23; 18:35; 19:36). Could it be that Jesus and the disciples' journey to Jerusalem symbolically embodies restored Israel's journey or "way" to the promised land, fulfilling Isaiah's promise? It makes sense, then, that Luke would allocate nearly

---

the fall, humanity's central problem is sin, not exile, for exile is a result of sin. See the discussion in G. K. Beale and Benjamin L. Gladd, *The Story Retold: A Biblical-Theological Introduction to the New Testament* (Downers Grove, IL: IVP Academic, 2020), 248–52.

16 Luke, more than the other three Evangelists, often refers to Jesus as "Lord" (1:15–17, 32, 38, 43; 2:9, 11; 3:4; 4:8; 5:8, 12; 6:5; 7:6; 9:54; etc.). The significance is that Luke undoubtedly presents Jesus as Israel's God incarnate. See discussion in Benjamin L. Gladd, *Handbook on the Gospels* (Grand Rapids, MI: Baker Academic, 2021), 215, 218, 231–232, 245, 281, 287, 303; C. Kavin Rowe, *Early Narrative Christology: The Lord in the Gospel of Luke*, BZNW 2/139 (New York: de Gruyter, 2006).

a third of his narrative to Jesus the incarnate Lord and a new Moses figure[17] leading his people out of spiritual bondage and into the new creation by his death and resurrection.

The first section of Luke (1:5–9:50) introduces the audience to the nature of Jesus's identity and the end-time kingdom, whereas the teaching on the road to Jerusalem explores the challenges and sacrifices believers will face if they desire to follow Jesus of Nazareth to the promised land of the new creation. We can break down the teaching into three general sections: expansion of the kingdom (10:1–11:13), inevitable conflict with the kingdom (11:14–54), and life within the kingdom (12:1–19:44).

Generally speaking, understanding and obedience do *not* mark this journey to Jerusalem. Indeed, the bulk of Jesus's parables are found here and, with them, the unbelief of the Jewish leaders and many within the crowds (e.g., 10:25–36; 11:14–23, 29–32, 37–54; 12:1–21; 14:1–6). Jesus's teaching and actions, too, frustrate the disciples, who often have difficulty grasping their meaning (9:45; 18:34).

The Journey from Jerusalem to Emmaus[18]

Jesus's second journey, the movement from Jerusalem to Emmaus (Luke 24:13–35), repeats the first journey from Galilee to Jerusalem but with a stark difference: the disciples now understand the totality of Jesus's ministry. In the first journey, the disciples struggled to comprehend the nature of the various aspects of Jesus's ministry, particularly his death and resurrection. But on the road to Emmaus, Jesus graciously gives his disciples eyes to see and ears to hear. He reverses the language of Isaiah 6:9–10 (see discussion in chapter 3).

---

17 Joel B. Green argues, "Luke has built up a series of reminiscences, some linguistic and others conceptual, of Exodus material . . . but he has done so in a way that mimics the Deuteronomic portrayal of the Exodus journey as a series of speeches delivered by Moses to the people of God" (Joel B. Green, *The Gospel of Luke*, NICNT [Grand Rapids, MI: Eerdmans, 1997], 398).

18 Portions of this section excerpted and adapted from pages 300–302 of *Handbook on the Gospels* by Benjamin L. Gladd, copyright © 2021. Used by permission of Baker Academic, a division of Baker Publishing Group.

To state the matter succinctly, the road to Emmaus tangibly demonstrates how Jesus's life, death, and resurrection fulfill the entire sweep of redemptive history (see Luke 1:1–4).

Two of Jesus's disciples, Cleopas and an unnamed disciple, were "talking with each other about all these things that had happened" (24:14). Jesus approached them, but they initially failed to recognize him, for "their eyes were kept from recognizing him" (24:16). Their lack of recognition stems from spiritual stubbornness, diagnosed by Jesus as slowness of heart to believe the Scriptures (24:25). But, ultimately, God is the one who withheld full comprehension of Jesus's identity. The two disciples, although they witnessed Jesus's miracles and listened to countless parables, have yet to grasp his identity in its fullness. The two also appear to be among those who distrust the women's report about Jesus's resurrection (24:11) and, ultimately, disbelieve Jesus's repeated passion predictions (9:22, 44; 12:50; 13:32–33; 17:25; 18:32–33; cf. 24:44).

The disciples are "looking sad" in 24:17 because their outward appearance manifests the condition of their heart. All hope appears lost. We have reached a fundamental problem in Luke's narrative. Jesus staked his mission on his resurrection. If he is not raised, then there's no redemption, no forgiveness of sins for Jews and Gentiles, no restoration of end-time Israel, nothing to rejoice over, no kingdom, no Messiah, no success as the Son of Man, no undoing of the first Adam's failure, and no fulfillment of the long-awaited promises of a second exodus.

Jesus asks the two followers what they are discussing. To their surprise, he seems to remain ignorant of what transpired in Jerusalem the last few days. In Luke 24:19–24 they recount Jesus's career, especially Passion Week. They confess that he "was a prophet mighty in deed and word before God and all the people" (24:19; cf. Acts 7:22), that the Jewish leaders "delivered him up to be condemned to death, and crucified," and that his followers "had hoped that he was the one to redeem Israel" (Luke 24:20–21). The disciples' appraisal of Jesus is not altogether incorrect. Indeed, they put their finger on a handful of important aspects of his identity—Jesus is a mighty prophet (Luke 4:14, 24; Acts 2:22), and the Jewish leaders did betray him (Luke 23:1–2). But they pine for a Messiah who will liberate them from Rome, not one who is characterized by suffering and bearing God's curse. The two disciples, too, fail to mention Jesus as Israel's "Lord."

THE DISCIPLES' INABILITY TO PERCEIVE
JESUS'S ACTS OF REDEMPTION

Jesus's strong reaction to the disciples' failure to grasp his identity is no small matter. Notice how Jesus castigates the disciples: "O foolish ones, and *slow of heart* to believe all that the prophets have spoken!" (24:25). The two disciples do not "believe" in their "hearts." The phrase "slow of heart" is key here. Mark (and Matthew to a lesser degree) underscores the spiritual obstinacy of the disciples throughout his account. The twelve are unable to perceive fully the nature of Jesus's identity and the end-time kingdom (Matt. 13:1–52; Mark 4:1–34). Luke, though, while he quotes Isaiah 6:9 in Luke 8:10, refrains from applying the disciples' ignorance until the end of his Gospel. There are pockets of ignorance, of course (see 9:45; 18:34), but the explicit obduracy language of "seeing" and hard "heart" and its connection to Isaiah 6 as it relates to the disciples is notably absent in the Third Gospel *until* Luke 24.[19] The presence of sensory language (see 24:16,

---

19 Commentators often neglect to connect the disciples' obduracy in Luke 24 with Isa. 6:9–10, probably because Luke doesn't explicitly quote Isa. 6 there. However, Isa. 6:9–10 stands behind the language of "heart" and "eyes" in Luke 24:16, 25, 31–32, 45 for four reasons: (1) Luke explicitly quotes Isa. 6:9 in Luke 8:10, a passage that includes the Isaianic language of "seeing" (*blepō*), "hearing" (*akouō*), and "understanding" (*syniēmi*). (2) According to Luke 24:45, Jesus "opened" the disciples' "minds *to understand* [*synienai*] the Scriptures." The same word, *syniēmi*, is found in both 8:10 and 24:45. (3) Luke quotes all of Isa. 6:9–10 in Acts 28:26–27, where the full list of sensory faculties is mentioned: "eyes," "ears," and "heart." So Luke demonstrates keen awareness of Isa. 6 because he quotes from Isa. 6 *twice* in his two-volume project, increasing the likelihood of the presence of Isa. 6 in Luke 24. (4) From a conceptual standpoint, sensory language found on the road to Emmaus in Luke 24 corresponds well with Isaiah's theology of obduracy and God's promise to reverse it (see discussion below).

25, 31–32, 45) is noteworthy and likely alludes to the prophet's commission of judgment in Isaiah 6 (see also Acts 28:26–27, quoting Isa. 6:9–10). See table 4.1.

Table 4.1   Comparison of Luke 24 and Isaiah 6:9–10

Luke 24	Isaiah 6:9–10
24:16 But their *eyes* [*hoi ophthalmoi*] were kept from recognizing him.	"'Keep on hearing, but do not understand;
24:25 And he said to them, "O foolish ones, and slow of *heart* [*tē kardia*] to believe all that the prophets have spoken!"	keep on seeing, but do not perceive.' Make the *heart* [*kardia*] of this people dull,
24:31–32 And their *eyes* [*hoi ophthalmoi*] were opened, and they recognized him. And he vanished from their sight. They said to each other, "Did not our *hearts* [*hē kardia*] burn within us while he talked to us on the road, while he opened to us the Scriptures?"	and their ears heavy, and blind their *eyes* [*tous ophthalmous*]; lest they see *with their eyes* [*tois ophthalmois*], and hear with their ears, and *understand* [*synōsin*] with their *hearts* [*tē kardia*],
24:45 Then he opened their minds *to understand* [*synienai*] the Scriptures.	and turn and be healed."

According to Luke 24:16, the two disciples are unable to perceive Jesus's true identity as the suffering Messiah and resurrected Lord. Later, in 24:25, the disciples lack the ability to understanding Jesus's identity in light of the Old Testament. For us to better appreciate the weight of this sensory language in the Third Gospel, we must briefly turn to the Old Testament.

ISRAEL'S INABILITY TO PERCEIVE GOD'S
FIRST AND SECOND EXODUSES

One of Isaiah's salient themes throughout the book is Israel's current state of obduracy on account of her idolatry (see, e.g., Isa. 6:9–10; 64:3–4). Israel isn't simply hardened in a general sense. As several texts within the book of Isaiah and elsewhere demonstrate, *the Israelites are hardened toward God's acts of redemption.* That is, they lack the spiritual ability to perceive the true meaning of God's actions. In the first exodus, God hardened Israel; her rebellious behavior prevented perception. Deuteronomy 29:2-4 functions as the fountainhead of this theme:

> Moses summoned all Israel and said to them: "You have seen all that the LORD did before your eyes in the land of Egypt, to Pharaoh and to all his servants and to all his land, the great trials that your eyes saw, the signs, and those great wonders. But to this day *the LORD has not given you a heart to understand or eyes to see or ears to hear.*"

The combination of "heart," "eyes," and "ears" often becomes stock language for idolatry.[20] Furthermore, the Deuteronomy passage affirms Israel's perception of God's mighty deeds yet without understanding. Psalm 106:7 is also worth citing in this regard:

> Our ancestors in Egypt *did not grasp*
> *the significance* of your wondrous works
> or remember your many acts of faithful love;
> instead, they rebelled by the sea—the Red Sea. (CSB)

On a surface level, Israel clearly comprehended Yahweh's unique status as she experienced his might in the exodus, but the nation remained calloused toward the spiritual "significance" of God's plans (see Ex. 32:4, 9, 30; Num. 14:22-35; Deut. 1:26-27, 43; 4:3). The book of Isaiah picks up and develops this theme—Israel's lack of spiritual perception toward God's redemptive activity. Isaiah looks back on how Israel failed to perceive God's actions in the first exodus (e.g., Isa. 42:18-20; 63:10) and expects that the majority of the Israelites will once again be spiritually obdurate in the second exodus (Isa. 64:3-4).[21] In brief, only

---

20 See especially the discussion in G. K. Beale, *We Become What We Worship: A Biblical Theology of Idolatry* (Downers Grove, IL: IVP Academic, 2008), 36–70.

21 Isaiah 64:3-4, a notoriously difficult passage, indicates that Israel was in a hardened state in the first exodus. They outwardly perceived God's unique status during the first exodus

a remnant of Israelites will grasp Yahweh's work of redemption in the second, eschatological exodus.

JESUS REVERSES THE DISCIPLES' OBDURACY

Now that we have a better handle on the Old Testament background of obduracy, we can more fully appreciate Jesus's actions with his disciples. He refuses to leave them in their ignorance in the second half of Luke 24. Daylight is quickly fading, so the two disciples ask Jesus to dine with them at an unknown residence (24:28–29; cf. John 20:19–23). As Jesus reclined, "he took the bread and blessed and broke it and gave it to them" (Luke 24:30). Luke's words are nearly identical to what we find at the Last Supper in 22:19, a covenant meal where Jesus explicitly predicts his suffering. At this moment, the two followers immediately realize Jesus's identity as their suffering king: "And their eyes *were opened*, and they recognized him" (24:31). The passive voice of the verb "were opened" (*diēnoichthēsan*) is probably a divine passive, where God is the agent (like "kept from" [ESV] or "prevented from" [CSB] in 24:16, cf. 24:45). God is the one who opens the disciples' minds for a correct understanding of Jesus (see Acts 16:14). This is an important point for Luke's readers, as they must recognize that their grasp of Jesus's life, death, and resurrection is ultimately a divine gift.

Jesus isn't done, though, with reversing the callousness of his disciples. Later, the two disciples arrive in Jerusalem and join the eleven (Luke 24:33). Jesus appears to the group and displays his scarred hands and feet that testify to his death (24:39–40). Then, he "*opened* [*diēnoixen*] their minds to understand the Scriptures" (24:45), the very

---

but did not truly understand God's redemptive actions. This passage also anticipates Israel's lack of perception in the future, second exodus. Paul quotes Isa. 64:4 in 1 Cor. 2:9, where he typologically applies the Isaianic passage to the "rulers of this age" (1 Cor. 2:8). Israel's limited and superficial understanding of God in the first exodus is a type of Israel's calloused perception in the second exodus. Paul is contrasting the rulers' lack of perception of God's redemptive plan in the wisdom of the cross (1 Cor. 2:7–9) with the spiritual insight of the Spirit-filled believer (1 Cor. 2:10–16). See the discussion in Benjamin L. Gladd, *Revealing the* Mysterion: *The Use of Mystery in Daniel and Second Temple Judaism with Its Bearing on First Corinthians;* BZNW 160 (Berlin: Walter de Gruyter, 2008, 139–48).

Scriptures that testify that he "should suffer and on the third day rise from the dead, and that repentance for the forgiveness of sins should be proclaimed in his name to all nations, beginning from Jerusalem" (24:46–47). Jesus reverses the Isaiah 6 obduracy on both levels; there's a wonderful symmetry in Jesus's miraculous work of healing the disciples' blindness. In Luke 24:16, the two disciples were blind to his identity, and in 24:25 they were blind to his identity with regard to the Old Testament. He then heals the disciples' blindness of his identity in 24:31 and removes the scales from their eyes in reading the Old Testament correctly in 24:45.

Jesus's actions with the disciples make wonderful sense in light of our discussion. Luke has kept his readers' attention squarely on Jesus's inauguration of the long-awaited Isaianic new exodus throughout his narrative. The disciples, though, lack *full* comprehension of Jesus's identity and, in particular, of how his death and resurrection relate to the new exodus. Only when Jesus opens their eyes do they come to grips with Jesus's identity and mission *and* how the Old Testament relates to him.

According to Isaiah 35, a passage concerning Israel's pilgrimage along the highway to the promised land of the new creation, the "eyes of the blind *shall be opened* [LXX: *anoichthēsontai*], and the ears of the deaf unstopped" (Isa. 35:5). Jesus quoted this very passage to John's disciples earlier in Luke 7:22 to validate his messianic ministry. Now, Jesus continues to fulfill the expectation of Isaiah 35 when he opens the eyes of his disciples. *Not only does Jesus spiritually restore his disciples for entrance into the promised land of the new creation, but he also enables them to grasp its significance.*[22] The disciples experience the long-awaited new exodus by trusting in and identifying with Jesus's life, death, and resurrection, and now they enjoy the spiritual perception of their personal exodus.

---

22 This identical theme of spiritually perceiving the significance of Jesus's inauguration of the new exodus is explicit in John's Gospel, where seven "signs" are catalogued. The signs of the first exodus typologically correspond to the seven signs of the Fourth Gospel. These seven signs manifest Jesus's identity as the glorious divine Son of God and result in giving the Father glory, eliciting belief or further unbelief, and accomplishing the redemption of his people (see John 2:1–11; 4:43–54; 5:1–15; 6:1–15; 9:1–12; 11:1–44; 19:1–20:31).

The Church as the "Way" to the Promised Land

According to Acts, believers are viewed as belonging to a group enigmatically called "the Way":

> But Saul . . . asked [the high priest] for letters to the synagogues at Damascus, so that if he found any belonging to *the Way* [*tēs hodou*], men or women, he might bring them bound to Jerusalem. (Acts 9:1–2)

> About that time there arose no little disturbance concerning *the Way* [*tēs hodou*]. (Acts 19:23)

> I [Paul] persecuted this *Way* [*tēn hodon*] to the death, binding and delivering to prison both men and women. (Acts 22:4; cf. 19:9)

> But this I [Paul] confess to you, that according to *the Way* [*tēn hodon*], which they call a sect, I worship the God of our fathers. (Acts 24:14)

The description of the Way echoes Isaiah 40–66, wherein, as I have discussed, God leads his people out of Babylonian exile and into the promised land on a "way" or "highway" (see, e.g., Isa. 11:16; 40:3; 43:19). Luke capitalizes on Isaiah's language and labels the early Christian movement as participating in the Way. God is, indeed, spiritually leading his people, the new Israel composed of Jews and Gentiles, out of exile and into the promised land. David Pao rightly suggests,

> In the narrative of Acts, the absolute use of the way-terminology again evokes the Exodus tradition in an attempt to (re)define the people of God and to establish the identity of the early Christian movement against the competing claims of the other party that also claims to share the ancestral tradition of Israel.[23]

---

23 David W. Pao, *Acts and the Isaianic New Exodus* (Grand Rapids, MI: Baker Academic, 2002), 66.

The first generation of Christians understood the significance of Jesus's leading his people out of spiritual captivity and into the promised land and chose to identify with it.

Traveling on the Way

How does one participate in the Way? Jesus inaugurates the second exodus, and the early church identified itself with it. But how do individuals travel on the way of life? I discussed at the end of chapter 3 that one enters into the covenant community by faith in Christ, and here I am asking a related question. What does life look like on the journey? What does it mean to follow the Son of Man throughout the totality of one's life? While there are several ways to sketch discipleship in Luke's Gospel, I will focus on a single group of individuals.

Three women—Mary Magdalene, Joanna, and Susanna—surface in Luke 8, and all share something in common: they "had been healed of evil spirits and infirmities" (8:2; cf. 7:21; 11:26). It is not entirely clear what is meant by "healed of evil spirits." Luke could be referring to the means by which Satan and his demons afflict humanity as a result of the fall (sickness, disease, etc.). At the very least, Luke suggests that nothing can impede the advancement and extent of the kingdom, not even Satan himself. The women are also named, perhaps demonstrating that they eventually testified about large portions of Jesus's ministry. The Evangelists often name individuals, especially women, in their narratives to disclose the source of their eyewitness accounts. We also learn that the women support Jesus and the disciples, probably financially: "[they] provided for them out of their means" (8:3). The same principle that is on display in 7:36–50 likely operates here: these women have been forgiven much, so they love much (7:41–47).

Importantly, Luke's narrative mentions Mary Magdalene and Joanna in two passages: 8:1–3 and 24:10. Richard Bauckham insightfully suggests that the two lists of names form an *inclusio* of sorts, "reminding the reader that the women's discipleship thus spans the whole narrative from chapter 8 to chapter 24."[24] If Bauckham is correct, then these women follow Jesus from Galilee, along the "way" to Jerusalem, throughout Passion Week in Jerusalem, and, climactically, to the tomb.

Perhaps we can extract a couple of principles of discipleship from these women: (1) It is often recognized that outsiders or sinners in Luke's Gospel participate in the kingdom and readily join themselves to Jesus. But some neglect to mention that outsiders must repent of their sinful past and change their selfish ways. These women embraced Jesus and concretely supported his ministry with their time, energy, and possessions. Discipleship, then, requires a turning *away* from sin and a devotion *to* the Son of Man (see, e.g., Luke 13:3; Acts 2:38; 3:19). (2) Apparently, these women continued to follow Jesus when all hope seemed lost. Though Luke doesn't explicitly mention the three women by name at the cross, his readers would certainly make this connection, as Luke 23:49 states, "The women who had followed him from Galilee stood at a distance watching these things [the events of the crucifixion]." The geographic detail "at a distance" may entail a reticence in their devotion to Jesus (cf. 22:54). But the women press on and later that day "followed" Joseph to the tomb (23:55–56). The point, then, is that following Jesus entails a lifelong commitment.

Conclusion

The exodus spans all of God's redemptive acts from Israel's deliverance from Egyptian bondage to the nation's entrance into the promised land. It lies at the heart of God's plan of redemption. Because of unbelief and rampant idolatry, God expelled Israel out of the promised land. But on account of his covenant with the patriarchs, the Old Testament prophets predicted that God would once again redeem his people and bring them back into the promised land through an eschatological second exodus. The Gospels expressly claim that Jesus of Nazareth fulfills the Old Testament expectation of a second exodus, and Luke's Gospel,

---

24 Richard Bauckham, *Gospel Women: Studies of the Named Women in the Gospels* (Grand Rapids, MI: Eerdmans, 2002), 113.

in particular, fashions a great deal of his material in accordance with this theme. Luke's two journeys correspond to Israel's journey in the wilderness. Whereas unbelief and confusion mark the journey to Jerusalem (Luke 9:51–19:27), belief and enlightenment define the journey to Emmaus (24:13–35). The disciples finally come to grips with Jesus's identity in light of the Old Testament and with their own redemption.

The church today must return again and again to the Scriptures and study Israel's exodus from Egyptian captivity. Without such knowledge, the church will not be able to comprehend its own redemption in Christ. The first exodus foreshadows Christ's work and gives believers confidence that God will "bring it to completion at the day of Jesus Christ" (Phil. 1:6).

5

The Success of the Last Adam

WITH THE EXCEPTION OF THE CROSS and resurrection, few events in Jesus's career are as critical as his wilderness temptation. In some sense, nearly every aspect of Jesus's earthly ministry can find its point of origin in the temptation. While the birth narratives and the last week of Jesus's ministry receive a great deal of attention, there's a reason why the Gospels dedicate so much material to the events between Jesus's birth and Passion Week.

The Synoptic Gospels follow the same general order: John baptizes Jesus in the Jordan River (Matt 3:13–17; Mark 1:9–11; Luke 3:21–22) and then Jesus immediately enters the Judean wilderness where Satan tempts him (Matt. 4:1–11; Mark 1:12–13; Luke 4:1–13). Then, Jesus preaches the arrival of the kingdom (Matt. 4:12–17; Mark 14–15; Luke 4:14–30). Luke, though, uniquely inserts a genealogy between Jesus's baptism and temptation (Luke 3:23–38) and places Jesus's rejection in Nazareth after the temptation (4:14–30). The point is clear: Jesus's baptism and subsequent temptation in the wilderness spearhead his ministry of redemption. The apostle Paul states that "all the promises of God find their Yes in [Christ]" (2 Cor. 1:20). That is, every single Old Testament promise, every historical pattern (persons, events, etc.), and each institution point to Jesus. Therefore, we should expect that a great deal of the Old Testament flows *through* the wilderness temptation. If the temptation didn't bear this much weight, then we would expect one of the Synoptics to omit it or allocate it to a different part of Jesus's career.

Our goal in this chapter is to examine Luke's presentation of the wilderness temptation and explore its significance for Jesus's life. One caveat before we begin our quest: I will endeavor to explain how the wilderness temptation fits within Luke's Gospel and Jesus's ministry at large. But the wilderness temptation is organically connected to Jesus's death and resurrection. What Jesus initially accomplishes in the wilderness he further achieves at the cross and resurrection. Then, when he returns a second time at the end of history, he will consummate the salvation he secured in his public ministry. Furthermore, when other New Testament authors refer to Christ's work, they often think in terms of Christ's ministry as a whole—from his birth to his exaltation (e.g., Rom. 1:1–4). Parsing the significance of Jesus's wilderness temptation *apart* from this death and resurrection is, therefore, a theologically difficult endeavor.

Preparations for Battle

Matthew and Luke are the only two Gospels that formally list Jesus's genealogy. One would expect Luke to place the genealogy before Jesus's birth like Matthew (Matt. 1:1–17), or before Jesus dialogues with the Jewish leaders as a twelve-year old boy in the temple, or even before Jesus's baptism. But Luke inserts the genealogy *between* Jesus's baptism and wilderness temptation (Luke 3:23–38). In addition to placement, there are also differences within the two genealogies. Matthew traces Jesus's lineage to the famed patriarch Abraham (Matt. 1:1), whereas Luke goes all the way back to Adam (Luke 3:38). Furthermore, Matthew proceeds from Abraham to Jesus, but Luke inverts the order, listing Jesus first and then finishing the genealogy with several names found in Israel's primeval history in Genesis 1–11 (Luke 3:35–38). Luke carefully connects the person of Jesus to the beginning of humanity. In doing so, Luke explicitly connects the wilderness temptation with Adam: "the son of Enos, the son of Seth, the *son of Adam*, the son of God. And Jesus, full of the Holy Spirit, returned from the Jordan and was led by the Spirit in the wilderness" (3:38–4:1). Clearly, Luke invites his readers to see Jesus's wilderness temptation through the lens of Adam's testing in the garden.

The last battery of names—Shem, Noah, Enoch, Seth, and Adam—is critical, as Luke guides his audience through the maze of people in the Genesis narrative and zeroes in on the godly line. According to Genesis 3:15, all of humanity is divided into two categories—the godly seed and the ungodly seed:

> I will put enmity between you [the serpent] and the woman [Eve],
>> and between your offspring and her offspring;
> he shall bruise your head,
>> and you shall bruise his heel.

The seed of the serpent and the seed of the woman are entangled with one another, and the two lines will continually wage war against one another until the end of history, when, according to Genesis 3:15, a godly king, in the pristine, perfected image of God, will vanquish the serpent, the embodiment of evil. Therefore, Luke draws from Genesis 1–3 to convince his readers that Jesus is the long-awaited King who will wage a definitive battle against the serpent. To appreciate Jesus's actions more fully in the wilderness, I must first take a moment and briefly develop an important dimension to Israel and her promised land.

God created Adam and Eve in his image (Gen. 1:26–28), and central to imaging God on earth is the first couple's prerogative to rule on behalf of God. Stated simply, God rules over the cosmos from his heavenly throne and commands Adam and Eve to rule over the earth as his vice-regents. So when the serpent enters the garden (Gen. 3:1), Adam and Eve should have immediately subdued the serpent and exterminated it. They did not, of course, and Adam and Eve subsequently succumbed to sin.

This same pattern is picked up when God commands the nation of Israel, a corporate Adam (Ex. 4:22; Hos. 6:7), to enter into the promised land. The promised land, too, should be broadly viewed as a garden of Eden (Ex. 15:17) and a microcosm of the entire cosmos. Just as Adam and Eve were to subdue all forms of idolatry and rebellion in the garden, so too the Israelites were to defeat the idolatrous people groups that inhabited the land. Despite several victorious military campaigns, the Israelites did not exterminate all their enemies from the promised land but eventually fell prey to syncretism (Judg. 2:10–12). As punishment for persistent idolatry, God exiled his people from the land. The Assyrians captured the northern tribes of Israel and enslaved them (2 Kings 17:5–6) in 722 BC, and later the Babylonians exiled the two southern tribes in 587/86 BC (2 Kings 23:26–27). Israel remained in exile for nearly seventy years until Cyrus decreed that Israel could return (2 Chron. 36:21–23; Ezra 1:1–4). When the nation of Israel returned, though, she did so under the political thumb of Persia. And although there were periods of independence, the nation remained under the control of foreigners into the first century AD.

First-century Jews pined for political independence—when the surrounding nations would bow the knee to Yahweh and his Messiah. What is so striking about Jesus's ministry is his insistence that his kingdom is "not of this world" (John 18:36). Jesus perceives the true threat to the Israelites—and to all of humanity for that matter. As wicked and idolatrous as Rome is, Caesar isn't Israel's archenemy. That distinction belongs to the devil himself. After formally identifying himself as true Israel in his baptism (Luke 3:21–22), Jesus's first act is to wage war against the serpent. The failure of Adam in the garden and Israel in the promised land prophetically anticipates Jesus's success in the wilderness.

Recall in 1:31 where the angel Gabriel instructs Mary to name her baby Jesus (1:31)—that is, *Iēsous*, the Greek rendering of the Hebrew name Joshua. Why? Because this reference to the prominent Old Testament figure of Joshua demonstrates that Jesus is the long-awaited ruler of God's people and the consummate priest-king who rules over God's enemies and expels them from his domain. The angel Gabriel also relates to Mary that Jesus "will be called the Son of the Most High.

And the Lord God will give to him the throne of *his father David*, and he will reign over the house of Jacob forever, and of his kingdom there will be no end" (1:32–33). Then, a few verses later, Gabriel explains, "The child to be born will be called holy—*the Son of God*" (1:35). Notice how Christ's identity as God's Son is wedded to kingship and the arrival of the eternal kingdom.[1]

Sonship and bearing God's image are nearly synonymous in the Bible. There are also several prominent Old Testament texts (see, e.g., 2 Sam. 7; Isa. 9:6) that tap into this theme and likely stand behind Gabriel's prophecy. In the first temptation, the devil tells Jesus, "If you are *the Son of God*, command this stone to become bread" (Luke 4:3). The point is that Jesus's identity as Israel's King comes to the fore in the temptation. *Therefore, in light of the broad contours of the story-line of the Old Testament and the first few chapters of Luke, we must view Jesus's activity in the wilderness as a cosmic battle.* The wilderness temptation is unique in that the Evangelists only mention Jesus—the Spirit-empowered King—and the devil involved in this war. They breathe not a whisper about physical or spiritual onlookers. Much like David and Goliath, this is a battle between the righteous one (and all those whom he corporately represents) and the unrighteous one (and all those whom he corporately represents).

The Wilderness Testing or Temptation?

Jesus appears as a passive figure, whereby the devil catches Jesus off guard and capitalizes on his dire situation, but the opposite is true. Luke 4 opens with the following: "Jesus, *full of the Holy Spirit . . .* was led *by the Spirit* in the wilderness" (4:1). Like every aspect of Jesus's

---

1   Meredith Kline rightly connects Jesus's birth in Luke 1 with the creation narrative in Gen. 1: "The Lucan birth narrative throws an interesting light on the overarching creative presence of the Glory-Spirit in Genesis 1. Luke records Gabriel's words to Mary in which the origin of the second Adam is attributed to the overshadowing presence and power of the Glory-Spirit (as was the case with the first Adam) and the explanation for calling the holy one thus produced the Son of God is found in this special creative involvement of the Glory-Spirit (Luke 1:35)" (*Kingdom Prologue: Genesis Foundations for a Covenantal Worldview* [Eugene, OR: Wipf & Stock, 2006], 45).

career, God purposed this event in eternity past. The devil may believe that he is initiating the contest with Jesus, but in reality everything is unfolding precisely the way God intended before time began.

All three Synoptics state that the devil "tempted" (Gk. *peirazō*) Jesus (Matt. 4:1; Mark 1:13; Luke 4:2). Indeed, Matthew even labels the devil "the tempter" (*ho peirazōn*; Matt. 4:3). The semantic range of this word contains two levels of meaning: (1) "to endeavor to discover the nature or character of someth[ing] by testing" and (2) "to entice to improper behavior."[2] Given the Old Testament background to Jesus's wilderness temptation in the Synoptics, one could argue that the devil is "testing" Jesus. Within the scope of the first definition, over and over again, the Old Testament generally refers to the second definition and maintains that God and he alone is the one who "tests" Israel in the exodus and wilderness wanderings (see Gen. 22:1; Ex. 15:25; 16:4; 20:20; Deut. 8:16; 13:3; Judg. 2:22; 3:1, 4; 2 Chron. 32:31; Ps. 26:2; Dan. 1:12, 14). If someone attempts to flip the script and "test" God, then God responds in judgment.[3]

What does it mean that God "tested" his people? The answer is disclosed in Deuteronomy 8:2: "And you shall remember the whole way that the LORD your God has led you these forty years in the wilderness, that he might humble you, *testing* you to know what was in your heart, whether you would keep his commandments or not." Testing reveals the motivation or inner disposition of one's heart. It determines whether one will obey or disobey God's law. Daniel Block comments on this passage, "Yahweh was testing his people to assess the quality of the vassal's fidelity (8:2) and to enhance Israel's covenant commitment through discipline (8:5)."[4] Such a definition explains why individuals must never test God, as God's faithfulness to his promises is unwavering (see Luke 4:12, quoting Deut. 6:16).[5]

---

2   "Πειράζω," BDAG 793.

3   See Ex. 17:2, 7; Num. 14:22–23; Pss. 78:18, 41, 56; 95:8–9; 106:14; cf. Isa. 7:12.

4   Daniel I. Block, *Deuteronomy*, NIVAC (Grand Rapids, MI: Zondervan, 2004), 227.

5   D. A. Carson supports this line of thought when he comments, "For us to 'tempt' or 'test' God is wrong because it reflects unbelief or attempted bribery (Ex 17:2, 7 [Ps 95:9]; Dt 6:16 [Mt 4:7]; Isa 7:12; Ac 5:9; 15:10)" ("Matthew," in *The Expositor's Bible Commentary:*

Exodus 17 stands out as Israel's defiant act, wherein the people tested God. There the Israelites "grumbled against Moses," demanding that God give them water (Ex. 17:3). Their actions are defiant because they are questioning the character of God and his fidelity to the Abrahamic covenant. Moses famously strikes the rock and causes water to gush forth (Ex. 17:6). Then he names the place "Massah and Meribah, because of the quarreling of the people of Israel, and because they tested the LORD by saying, 'Is the LORD among us or not?'" (Ex. 17:7). The LXX translates this verse straightforwardly with the exception of the two place names: "And [Moses] called the name of that place, *Temptation* [*Peirasmos*], and Reviling" (Brenton). Few events in Israel's checkered history are as noteworthy as what took place here in Exodus 17. Indeed, the Old and New Testaments keep coming back to this specific incident of rebellion (see Num. 20:13; Deut. 6:16; 9:22; 33:8; Pss. 95:8; 106:32; 1 Cor. 10:4; Heb. 3:8).[6]

As we circle back to Luke 4, we stand aghast at the devil's conduct in testing Jesus. Yes, of course, on the one hand the devil is "enticing" or baiting Jesus to sin, but he is also "testing" the very identity of Jesus. The points of contact between Satan testing/tempting Jesus in the wilderness and God testing the Israelites are numerous, so the two definitions of *peirazō* may coalesce here. Perhaps the devil audaciously decides to "test" the Son of God to determine whether or not he would remain faithful in trusting in the Father's provision. In Israel's exodus from Egypt and throughout the wilderness temptation, God tested Israel to determine whether she would cling to the promises of God. Now the devil assumes the role of God himself to see if Jesus would prove faithful. But there's yet another layer of theology at work. I mentioned above that God sovereignly planned that Jesus would endure the devil's advances. So the Father tests the Son by engineering the devil to test

---

Matthew–Mark, rev. ed., ed. Tremper Longman III and David E. Garland [Grand Rapids, MI: Zondervan, 2010], 140–41).

6 Note, too, that Ps. 78:56 states that the second generation of Israelites "tested" God when they entered the promised land: "Yet they tested and rebelled against the Most High God and did not keep his testimonies" (cf. Ps. 78:18, 41).

Jesus, knowing full well that the Son will pass the test.[7] This explains why the devil perhaps unwittingly imitates the Spirit. According to Luke 4:1, the Spirit "led" (*ēgeto*) Jesus into the wilderness. In 4:5 Satan "led" (NASB; *anagagōn*) Jesus to see the kingdoms of the world, and in 4:9 he "led" (NIV; *ēgagen*) Jesus to the temple in Jerusalem.[8]

The Three Temptations (4:1–13)

A detailed study of the three temptations is beyond the scope of this chapter. I discuss portions of Jesus's wilderness temptation in chapters 1 and 6, so I need not examine each passage in detail. Instead, I will endeavor to get a sense of each temptation and how each functions in Luke's broader context.

Luke states that Jesus was "led by the Spirit in the wilderness for forty days, being tempted by the devil" (4:1–2). Apparently, the devil confronts Jesus at the end of the forty-day fast, when Jesus is most vulnerable (see Matt. 4:2). But the ambiguous wording in Luke 4:2 that Jesus was in the wilderness for forty days "being tempted by the devil" may suggest that the devil had been assaulting Jesus the entire time and that the three temptations are the culmination of the attack.[9] In any case, all three Synoptics claim that Jesus was (1) in the wilderness (2) for forty days—two bits of information that clearly allude to Israel's wilderness wanderings.[10] Numbers 14:34 explains why Israel wandered so long: "According to the number of the days in which you spied out the land, forty days, a year for each day, you shall bear your iniquity forty years, and you shall know my displeasure" (cf. Ezek. 4:4–5). For

---

7   Carson comes to the same conclusion: "In Jesus' 'temptations' God clearly purposed to test him just as Israel was tested, and Jesus' responses prove that he understood" ("Matthew," 141).

8   According to the second and third temptations in Matthew's narrative, the devil "took" (*paralambanō*) Jesus to the desired location (Matt. 4:5, 8). But Luke's Gospel relates how the devil twice "led" Jesus (*anagō* /*agō*; 4:5, 9). Luke's narrative, then, may intentionally present the devil as imitating the Spirit in 4:1.

9   Demons are often associated with the wilderness in Second Temple Judaism (see 1 En. 10:4–5; 2 Bar. 10:8; Tob. 8:3; 4 Macc. 18:8; cf. LXX Isa. 13:21; 34:14).

10 Forty days may also recall other significant redemptive-historical events such as the flood (Gen. 8:6) and Moses's forty-day stint on Sinai when he fasts (Ex. 24:18; 34:28; Deut. 9:11).

each day the twelve Israelite representatives spied out the land, the first generation of Israelites restlessly wandered a year in the desert. Faithlessness and unbelief in God's promises characterize the wilderness in the Old Testament, actions that resulted in judgment and exile. Jesus, as the last Adam and true Israel, consciously retraces Israel's steps. His faithfulness and belief in God's promises result in restoration and life. Before I briefly examine the three temptations, here's an overview of Satan's threefold attack (see table 5.1):

Table 5.1   Satan's Commands to Jesus and the Implied Temptations

Satan's Commands	Temptation
"If you are the Son of God, command this stone to become bread" (Luke 4:3)	Doubt God's promises
"If you, then, will worship me, it will all be yours" (Luke 4:7)	Worship and submit to Satan
"If you are the Son of God, throw yourself down from here" (Luke 4:9)	Manipulate God

First Temptation (4:3–4)

In the first temptation, the devil tells Jesus, "If you are the Son of God, command this stone to become bread" (Luke 4:3 // Matt. 4:3). Due to the first-class conditional statement in Luke 4:3, the devil is not wondering if Jesus is the Son of God. Instead, the temptation is based on the truthfulness of that reality. *Because* Jesus is truly God's Son, the God-man (see 1:32, 35; 3:22), the devil tempts him to exploit his identity and transform the stone into bread. Why is this a temptation, and why does the devil lead his attack with this specific temptation? The answers are multifold.

The devil is tempting Jesus to do what his Father forbids. The Father hasn't willed for the Son to nourish himself but to rely on and trust in the Father's provision. To break his fast is tantamount to asserting his independence from the Father. On a redemptive-historical plane, this temptation evokes Adam and Eve's lack of trust in God. In the garden,

God commanded them what to do and what not to do. Positively, God commissioned the first couple to produce godly descendants, expand the boundaries of Eden, fill the earth with God's glory, keep his commands, and subdue evil (Gen. 1:26–28; 2:15, 24). Negatively, God prohibited Adam and Eve from partaking of the tree of the knowledge of good and evil (Gen. 2:17). In the end, they failed to obey both aspects of God's law. In short, they failed to trust God.

The same can be said for Israel wandering in the desert. Immediately following the Red Sea crossing and the Song of Moses (Ex. 13:17–15:21), the Israelites begin to grumble. At first, they grumble because of the absence of fresh water (Ex. 15:22–27), and then they grumble because of the lack of food (Ex. 16:2–3). So God graciously promises to feed them with "bread from heaven" or manna (Ex. 16:4). This act is a test for the Israelites: "I am about to rain bread from heaven . . . that I may test them, whether they will walk in my law or not" (Ex. 16:4). God's provision of manna for his people throughout the wilderness wanderings is one of the most significant events in Israel's history.[11] Manna tangibly symbolizes God's gracious and faithful character in providing for his people. Did the Israelites trust that God would provide for them daily and rain down manna on them? The answer is no. Neither the majority of the first generation of Israelites nor the majority of subsequent generations wholly believed that God would spiritually nourish them with his life-giving presence in the mobile tabernacle and meet their physical needs with manna (see, e.g., Num. 11:6–9).

So if Jesus were to transform the stone into bread, then he would lay aside his identity as true and faithful Adam/Israel and join every person before him in disobedience. To transform the stone into bread is to doubt the faithfulness and goodness of God. But if Jesus refuses to transform the stone into bread and waits for the Father to provide nourishment after the forty days of fasting, then Jesus will pass the test and will rest in the Father's provision. Jesus not only refuses to

---

11 See Deut. 8:3, 16; Josh. 5:12; Neh. 9:15–20; Ps. 78:24–25; John 6:31, 49; 1 Cor. 10:3.

fall prey to Satan's trap but also quotes from Deuteronomy 8 (italicized portion):

> And you [Israel] shall remember the whole way that the LORD your God has led you these forty years in the wilderness, that he might humble you, testing you to know what was in your heart, whether you would keep his commandments or not. And he humbled you and let you hunger and fed you with manna, which you did not know, nor did your fathers know, that he might make you know that *man does not live by bread alone*, but man lives by every word that comes from the mouth of the LORD. (Deut. 8:2–3)

In the book of Deuteronomy, Moses addresses the second generation of Israelites to avoid the behavior of the first generation. When the Israelites populate the promised land, a territory filled with agricultural abundance, they must never cease to depend on God's promises (see Deut. 8:16–18). As the true and faithful Adam/Israel, Jesus obeys God's command and "lives by every word" from the Father.

Second Temptation (4:5–8)

Why Luke and Matthew don't agree on the order of the second and third temptations is unclear.[12] In the second temptation, according to Luke, the devil took Jesus and "showed him all the kingdoms of the world in a moment of time" (Luke 4:5). Matthew's Gospel mentions that the devil "took" Jesus "to a very high mountain" (Matt. 4:8), a phrase that is reminiscent of apocalyptic settings (see Rev. 4:1; 17:3; 21:10). Marshall suggests that the second and third temptations took place in the form of a vision (Luke 4:5–8).[13]

The second temptation is predicated on the devil's possession of (1) authority over the kingdoms of the world and (2) the purported

---

12 John Nolland suggests that the order is reversed to highlight the city of Jerusalem, where Jesus is put to death (*Luke 1–9:20*, WBC [Grand Rapids, MI: Zondervan, 1989], 179).

13 I. Howard Marshall, *The Gospel of Luke: A Commentary on the Greek Text*, NIGTC (Grand Rapids, MI: Eerdmans, 1978), 171.

prerogative to hand over such authority to whomever he desires. The first claim appears generally true, as Scripture affirms that God, because of the fall, gave the devil the right to rule over the earth for a certain amount of time (e.g., Job 1:6–12; 2:17; John 12:31; 14:30; Rev. 12:7–12). But the devil's second assertion—the right to give the authority to whomever he wills—is fallacious. Nowhere in the Bible does Satan possess this prerogative, for that only belongs to Yahweh, the cosmic King. Such a claim is erroneous and audacious. I argue in chapter 6 that Satan subtly alludes to Daniel 7 and parodies the Ancient of Days here in the second temptation. The Ancient of Days entrusts the eternal kingdom to the son of man (Dan. 7:14) on account of his successful defeat of the fourth beast (Dan. 7:11). When the devil promises to hand over to Jesus the authority of the kingdoms of the world, he consciously steps into the divine role of the Ancient of Days.[14]

The devil's goal is for Jesus to "worship" (*proskyneō*) him. Worship in Luke 4:7 entails a two-pronged meaning: continual adoration and subordination (e.g., Gen. 27:29). So if Jesus "worships" the devil, then Jesus will assume a subordinate role to the devil and will operate under his command. The devil, though, receives a promotion of sorts in that he will govern the very Son of God. At first blush, it appears that Jesus will receive the better end of the deal (the right to rule over the earthly kingdoms), but in reality Satan does. If Jesus submits to the devil and inherits authority over the earthly domain, then doesn't the devil assume authority over Jesus and by implication the kingdoms?

Jesus responds with a citation from Deuteronomy 6:13.

It is written,

---

14 Commentators note the similarities between the second temptation and Moses "going up" to Mount Nebo, where God "showed" (*edeixen*) him the promised land in LXX Deut. 34:1–4 (see James Edwards, *The Gospel according to Luke*, PNTC [Grand Rapids, MI: Eerdmans, 2015], 129; David E. Garland, *Luke*, ZECNT [Grand Rapids, MI: Zondervan, 2011], 182). If the connection is legitimate, then these connections strengthen my argument that the devil consciously imitates God. In Deut. 34, Yahweh shows Moses the promised land, whereas in Luke 4, Satan shows Jesus.

> "You shall worship the Lord your God,
>   and him only shall you serve." (Luke 4:8)[15]

According to Deuteronomy 6:13, Israel must remain in submission to Yahweh's rule and maintain allegiance to him, despite pressure from the surrounding pagan nations (Ex. 20:5; 23:24). Exclusive worship of God separates Israel from all other nations. Monotheism is *the* defining attribute of Israel's religion (see Deut. 6:4; Isa. 42:8; Mark 12:29; 1 Cor. 8:4–6). Adam and Eve's decision to partake of the tree of the knowledge of good and evil (Gen. 3:6) is an attempt to cast off the divine image and become independent of God. They grew tired of submitting to God's rule; they desired to become the arbiters of right and wrong. Adam and Eve didn't bow down to physical idols but worshiped themselves—the most heinous form of idolatry. Likewise, Israel succumbed to idolatry by worshiping other gods (see, e.g., Ex. 32:8; cf. 34:14; Lev. 26:1; Num. 25:2; Deut. 4:19; 8:19; 11:16). This resulted in the Lord judging the nation and casting them into exile. Jesus repeats the same test but refuses to give in to Satan's devices.

As true and faithful Adam/Israel, Jesus upholds exclusive worship to his Father. Luke's Gospel contains three occurrences of the verb for "worship" (*proskyneō*). Two are found here in the temptation (Luke 4:7, 8); the third occurs at the end of the Gospel. Luke concludes with the account of Jesus's ascension into heaven, where the disciples "worshiped" (*proskynēsantes*) him (24:52). Reading this in light of the second temptation is staggering. Worship is reserved for Yahweh alone; therefore, if the disciples worship Jesus, then he must be identified with Yahweh. In the temptation narrative, Jesus, in his perfect humanity, worships the Father. At the end of the narrative, the disciples worship Jesus because he is also God. The human nature and divine nature come together in Jesus.

---

15 The quotation of Deut. 6:13 is slightly different from the LXX in that Jesus, as identically recorded in Matt. 4:10 and Luke 4:8, appears to amplify the command for Israel to worship God exclusively. Jesus replaces the word "fear" (*phobēthēsē*) with "worship" (*proskynēseis*) and then adds the word "only" (*monō*).

Third Temptation (4:9–12)

The third temptation is arguably the most sophisticated of the three, on account of the devil's citation of Psalm 91:11–12. Probably taking place in the form of a vision, Satan led Jesus to Jerusalem and "set him on the pinnacle of the temple" (Luke 4:9). The setting for the third and final temptation is natural because Israel's temple is an integral part of Jesus's ministry and because Jesus will spend his final week in Jerusalem (19:28–24:12). Like the first temptation, the devil's deception is once again predicated on the truthfulness of Jesus's identity as the Son of God. *Because* Jesus is God in the flesh and the true Adam/Israel, the devil tempts him to "throw [himself] down" from the ledge of the temple. Audaciously, the devil supports the temptation with a citation from Psalm 91:11–12:

> For it is written,
>
>> "He will command his angels concerning you,
>>   to guard you,"
>
> and
>
>> "On their hands they will bear you up,
>>   lest you strike your foot against a stone." (Luke 4:10–11)

Imitating Jesus's preface to his first two quotations from Deuteronomy (Luke 4:4, 8), Satan opens the psalm quotation with, "It is written." Like the second temptation, Satan appeals to the promises of God. Such a maneuver stands in contrast with his first temptation where he entices Jesus *not* to trust in God's promises. Satan's use of the Old Testament is layered with irony and misinterpretation, so unpacking it with care is difficult. Both parties wield Scripture as a weapon, but only one does so with hermeneutical integrity. However, I only need to address a few items in Satan's use of the psalm. For example, the devil reads

Psalm 91:11–12 too woodenly and narrowly. Psalm 91, which ensures God's protection of the righteous, makes no claim that God will spare his people from physical harm. The point is, as commentators often point out, that God will *spiritually* preserve the souls of the saints from injury.[16] In commanding angels to come to the rescue, the devil desires to control God's provision by compelling him to protect the Son. At the nub of this temptation, Satan desires for Jesus to manipulate his Father—to force his hand by sending his angels to preserve the Son. Leaping off the edge of the temple is not the will of the Father.

Jesus cites Scripture one last time: "It is said, 'You shall not put the Lord your God to the test'" (Luke 4:12, quoting Deut. 6:16). Here's the larger context:

> *You shall not put the Lord your God to the test*, as you tested him at Massah. You shall diligently keep the commandments of the Lord your God, and his testimonies and his statutes, which he has commanded you. And you shall do what is right and good in the sight of the Lord, that it may go well with you, and that you may go in and take possession of the good land that the Lord swore to give to your fathers by thrusting out all your enemies from before you, as the Lord has promised. (Deut. 6:16–19)

Deuteronomy 6:16 recalls Exodus 17:1–7, where, as I noted above, Israel demanded water from God and questioned his character. The context of Deuteronomy 6:16–19 is significant because it discloses the *goal* of Israel's obedience to God's will: "possession of the good land" and the extermination of the pagan inhabitants. Israel failed to obey the law of God, and though she crossed the Jordan and entered the promised land, she never took consummate possession of the land. Jesus, the perfect and true Israel, retraces the nation's steps and obeys the Father,

---

16 The promise of preservation is extended to the one who "dwells in the shelter of the Most High" (Ps. 91:1). The psalmist calls God the "Most High" twice (91:1, 9). Not coincidentally, Gabriel informs Mary that Jesus "will be called the Son of the Most High" and that "the power of the Most High will overshadow" her (Luke 1:32, 35; cf. 2:14; 6:35; 8:28; 19:38).

resulting in the subjugation of Israel's enemies. We must remember that the promised land is a microcosm of the entire cosmos. So, *as Jesus takes possession of the land, he's taking possession of the cosmos—physical and spiritual realms.*

The devil's quotation of Scripture is also filled with irony. Satan quotes Psalm 91:11–12, but he leaves out 91:13 which reads,

> You will tread on the lion and the adder;
> > the young lion and the serpent you will trample underfoot. (cf.
> > Deut. 8:15).

Psalm 91:13 even alludes to Genesis 3:15:

> I will put enmity between you [the serpent] and the woman [Eve],
> > and between your offspring and her offspring;
> he shall bruise your head,
> > and you shall bruise his heel.

While Satan applies the psalm too narrowly and ignores the promise of Ps 91:13, Jesus will indeed fulfill the typological expectation of Psalm 91.[17] By not following the devil's misuse of the psalm, he ironically preserves its true intent.

New Beginnings in the Wilderness

The wilderness is a rich subject, referring to a particular *time* in Israel's career and a unique *place*.[18] It often embodies God testing Israel and her idolatrous disobedience. But the wilderness isn't always pejorative in the Bible, as it can also refer to a wellspring of new beginnings.

---

17 The MT lacks a superscription for Psalm 91, whereas LXX (Psalm 90) adds that it is a "song of David." Assigning Davidic authorship to the psalm bolsters the case for a typological reading of it. The promise of God preserving his righteous servants in Psalm 91 is fulfilled in his preservation of Jesus in the wilderness temptation and throughout his earthly ministry.

18 Alison Schofield, "Wilderness," in *The Eerdmans Dictionary of Early Judaism*, ed. John J. Collins and Daniel C. Harlow (Grand Rapids, MI: Eerdmans, 2010), 1337.

Israel's exodus from Egypt, the giving of the law at Sinai, God's glory dwelling with his people, and the crossing of the Jordan all relate to the wilderness motif. Both dimensions of wilderness interlock here in Luke 4 but with a stark difference: instead of rampant distrust in God's promises, Jesus, the true and faithful Adam/Israel, steadfastly embraces the Father's will and passes the test. The unbelief and disobedience of Adam and Israel typologically anticipate Jesus's belief and obedience. The successful outcome of Jesus's testing results in the initial fulfillment of a large swath of Old Testament prophecy. Indeed, the wilderness temptation fulfills so many Old Testament anticipations that it is difficult to discuss what is *not* initially fulfilled.

While many more could be suggested, the following are three redemptive-historical trajectories that flow through Jesus's success in the wilderness (note that all three themes contain substantial overlap):

1. The second exodus. The second exodus, one of the most dominant expectations in the Old Testament, anticipates Yahweh's redeeming his people in the wilderness (see chapter 4). The Evangelists explicitly associate Isaiah 40:3 ("a voice cries: '*In the wilderness* prepare the way of the Lord'") with Jesus's baptism by John in the Jordan.[19] Watts, as mentioned in the previous chapter, rightly argues that the exodus "comprises three fundamental elements: Israel's deliverance from Egypt; the journey through the wilderness; and the arrival in the Promised Land."[20] Jesus's temptation touches on all three elements. He redeems his people *from* spiritual Egypt and installs them *in* the promised land *by* succeeding in his journey of obedience through the wilderness.

2. The new creation. Jesus's forty-day wilderness experience is the catalyst for the new creation. This explains why Jesus, immediately following the temptation, travels to Nazareth and declares the initial fulfillment of the eschatological year of jubilee (Luke 4:18–21, quoting Isa. 61:1–2).

---

19 See also Isa. 35:1–6; 41:18; 42:11; 43:19–20; 51:3; 62:4; Ezek. 36:35.

20 R. E. Watts, "Exodus," *New Dictionary of Biblical Theology*, ed. T. D. Alexander and B. S. Rosner, (Downers Grove, IL: IVP, 2000), 479.

3. King and kingship. Jesus's temptation also establishes the eternal kingdom and secures the enthronement of Israel's Messiah. G. K. Beale rightly asserts,

> Jesus's victory over temptation appears to have prepared him to conquer the one who was the ultimate satanic prince of the Canaanites and of all wicked nations and to conquer the land in a way that Israel had not been able to do. His very resistance to these satanic allurements was the very beginning of his defeat of the devil. Jesus's ministry of casting out demons continues his holy warfare as the true Israel. His exorcisms were an expression of his incipient, though decisive, defeat of Satan, who had brought creation into captivity through his deception of Adam and Eve.[21]

Who Is the Son of God?

Now that I have taken inventory of the wilderness temptation, I am in a better position to ask the all-important question of how the temptation narrative sheds light on Jesus's identity. The wilderness temptation attacks both natures of Jesus. First and foremost, the devil is enticing Jesus to sin in his human nature. We must always be mindful that Jesus is not simply a man. He is *the* perfect and true Adam and Israel. Jesus repeats the story of Adam and Israel but with remarkable success. Two important theological truths emerge in light of Jesus's success as the perfect Adam/Israel.

First, the wilderness temptation is the beginning of Jesus's fulfillment of the covenant of works—the same covenant that God made with Adam in the garden and generally with Israel at Sinai. The covenant of works concerns both positive and negative commands, for God tells Adam and Eve what to do and what not to do. They must rule as kings on God's behalf, fill the earth with his glory as priests, and embody and teach God's law to one another as prophets

---

21 G. K. Beale, *A New Testament Biblical Theology: The Unfolding of the Old Testament in the New* (Grand Rapids, MI: Baker Academic, 2011), 419–20.

(Gen. 1:26–28; 2:15; 2:24). They must also refrain from partaking of the tree of the knowledge of good and evil (Gen. 2:17), an idolatrous act that symbolized complete autonomy from God. Jesus initially fulfills both dimensions of the covenant of works in the wilderness temptation. He executed the threefold office of king, priest, and prophet. Jesus subdues evil, begins to fill the cosmos with God's glory, and faithfully embodies God's Word. He also refuses to act independently of the Father, which is the equivalent of partaking of the tree of knowledge of good and evil. At every point, Jesus submits to his Father's will.

Second, there are hints that the devil takes aim at Jesus's divine nature. For example, the title "Son of God" in Luke 4:3 and 4:8 likely refers to Jesus as the faithful Adam/Israel *and* the Father's divine Son. At some level, Jesus's sonship in all four Gospels often refers to his divine identity.[22] The first and third temptations are even predicated on Jesus's divine sonship. What difference does Jesus's divine identity make in the temptation? One critical Trinitarian principle is the unity between the three persons. For example, the Father, Son, and Spirit have a single will. Seen through this theological grid, the devil's trickery takes on an additional dimension. Satan is not only attempting to subvert Jesus's human dependence on the Father, but he is also attempting to create a breach within the Trinity when he entices Jesus to act on his own accord.

The Devil as Humanity's Slanderer

Our final reflection concerns the devil's identity in Luke 4. Matthew and Luke exclusively label the devil as *diabolos* in the wilderness temptation (Matt. 4:1, 5, 8, 11; Luke 4:2, 3, 6, 13). The loaded term *diabolos* consistently refers to an inimical figure in Israel's history who is characterized by slander and deception. Revelation 12:9–10 summarizes his character

---

22 Richard Bauckham claims that the title "Son of God" refers "not merely to a status or office to which Jesus is appointed but to a profound relationship that binds the Father and Son together" (*Who Is God? Key Moments of Biblical Revelation* [Grand Rapids, MI: Baker Academic, 2020], 98).

in the following way: "that ancient serpent, who is called *the devil* [*diabolos*] and *Satan* [*satanas*], the deceiver of the whole world . . . who accuses [the saints] day and night before our God." Deception and slander go hand in hand.[23] The Old Testament contains a handful of texts that describe the nature of the devil's schemes. The setting is often the divine council in heaven, where Satan legally prosecutes the saints of wrongdoing. The classic example is Job 1, where "Satan" (Heb. *hassatan*; Gk. *diabolos*) approaches the Lord and falsely accuses Job of lacking genuine faith (Job 1:9–11; cf. 2:4–5; 1 Kings 22:21–23). We discover a similar event in Zecheriah 3, when Satan stands at the right hand of Joshua the high priest to "accuse him" (Zech. 3:1; see also 1 Chron. 21:1).

Grasping the devil's twofold description as deceiver and slanderer further illuminates Luke's depiction of the wilderness temptation. If slandering the saints is one of Satan's chief characterizations, then perhaps the wilderness temptation touches on this theme. A clue is found in Luke 10:18, where Jesus "saw Satan fall like lightning" when the seventy-two disciples return. His "fall" from heaven in Luke 10 may refer, at some level, to the loss of his ability to slander and accuse the saints of wrongdoing in the divine courtroom (see Rev. 12:7–9). I argue in chapter 2 that the devil and his demons play a constitutive part in the fracturing of the nations and enticing them into idolatry. As a result of Jesus's inaugurating "peace" in heaven and on earth, division and idolatry no longer imprison humanity (Luke 2:14; 19:38), allowing the gospel to take root in the fertile soil of the nations.

At the end of the temptation, Luke is the only Evangelist to state, "And when the devil had ended every temptation, he departed from him until an opportune time" (4:13). This statement often confounds Luke's readers, but perhaps it partly refers to the devil's work of slander. Since Satan, the great "accuser" (*ho katēgōr*, Rev. 12:10), has lost his place

---

23 G. K. Beale argues that deception and slander operate in the garden, too, where the serpent's "claims that God's command to Adam and Eve in Gen. 2:16–17 is not true (Gen. 3:1, 4) and that God has deceptive motives in forbidding them to eat of the tree (Gen. 3:4–5) slander the character of God, and the serpent utilizes this slander to deceive the woman and the man" (*The Book of Revelation: A Commentary on the Greek Text*, NIGTC [Grand Rapids, MI: Eerdmans, 1999], 656).

in heaven where he slandered the saints before God, he transitions to slandering the saints before men. As Luke's Gospel unfolds, Satan works *through* many of the Jewish leaders to continue his warpath of destructive slander. In Luke 6:7 they even attempt "to accuse" (*katēgorein*) Jesus of disobeying God's law. Satan's ministry of slander culminates when he entered Judas (22:3) and then when he incited the Jewish leaders "to accuse" (*katēgorein*) Jesus of misleading Israel (23:2). The Jewish leaders ironically accuse Jesus of deceiving the people, when they themselves are the ones doing so. What about the cross? Doesn't the cross function as the zenith of the devil's slander? The Jewish leaders pursue death by crucifixion because it symbolizes sedition against Rome and because it symbolizes bearing God's covenant curse (see Gal. 3:13, quoting Deut. 21:23). Jesus is, of course, innocent of both. He is neither an insurrectionist nor a lawbreaker. But at the very heart of the gospel is a staggering truth: while Jesus is innocent of all false accusations, he willingly, for our sake, becomes the very thing he is falsely accused of!

Conclusion

The wilderness temptation, one of the most underappreciated events in the life of Christ, is layered with redemptive-historical profundity. It sets the trajectory for Jesus's ministry as the divine Son of God and the Son of Man. He achieves what no one else in history could achieve—absolute and perfect trust in God. Christ's success in the wilderness secures the birth of the eternal kingdom and the initial overthrow of the devil's reign. What Jesus initially accomplishes in the wilderness he achieves in a more escalated way at the cross and resurrection.

Those who rest in Christ's work in the wilderness temptation identify with his success. We overcome sin and temptation because of what he accomplished in the wilderness temptation and at the cross and resurrection. Jesus's victory in the wilderness also gives us a template of how believers defeat the devil on a personal level. Like Jesus, we must unswervingly trust the promises of God. Like Jesus, we must also know the Scriptures deeply and wield them carefully when Satan attacks.

6

The Son of Man's Rule and the Ancient of Days

JESUS'S FAVORITE TITLE, THE "SON OF MAN," occurs some eighty-one times in the Gospels, and all four Gospels knit this title into their tapestry of Jesus. Scholars of all stripes recognize the importance of the title, but no little debate has sprung forth from it.[1] Some contend that the phrase simply means "I."[2] But the Greek wording behind the "Son of Man" (*ho huios tou anthrōpou*) is quite enigmatic, meaning something to the effect of "the son of *the* man." Jesus is the "son" of what "man"? The title is also problematic because the vast majority of occurrences fall on the lips of Jesus himself; rarely does another party give Jesus that appellation (see John 12:34). Oddly, the only other portions of the New Testament that explicitly refer to Jesus as "the Son of Man" are Acts 7:56; Hebrews 2:6 (quoting Ps. 8:4); and Revelation 1:13 and 14:14 (both alluding to Dan. 7:13–14). Lastly, the phrase in the Gospels crops up on a few occasions in conjunction with Daniel 7 quotations (e.g., Matt. 24:30 // Mark 13:26 // Luke 21:27; Matt. 26:64 // Mark 14:62), and Daniel 7 itself is exceedingly difficult in its own right.

---

1 For a recent survey of the scholarly discussion of the "Son of Man," see Larry W. Hurtado and Paul L. Owen, eds., *'Who Is This Son of Man?': The Latest Scholarship on a Puzzling Expression of the Historical Jesus*, LNTS 390 (New York: T&T Clark, 2011).

2 E.g., Maurice Casey, *The Solution to the 'Son of Man' Problem* (New York: T&T Clark, 2009).

Commentators wrestle with the implications for the Son of Man sayings when they are wedded to Daniel 7 quotations. But, oddly, scholars often fail to connect the phrase to allusions to Daniel 7, and fewer tease out their significance. Our purpose here is not to examine every instance of the "Son of Man" in Luke's narrative but to recognize critical quotations *and* allusions to Daniel 7 in conjunction with the Son of Man. Daniel 7 contains a symbolic and dramatic story that lies at the heart of Jesus's ministry, and Luke keeps his audience attuned to this Danielic drama from start to finish. At five critical junctures within the Third Gospel, the Evangelist underscores the importance of this theme in his presentation of Jesus of Nazareth. Jesus opens his ministry, in fulfillment of Daniel 7, as the Son of Man approaching the Ancient of Days, and he closes his ministry with taking his seat on the very throne of the Ancient of Days. This is the most difficult chapter of this project, but its difficulty makes the identity of Jesus all the more enlightening.

Daniel 7 and the Son of Man[3]

Before we trace the uses of the "Son of Man" in Luke's Gospel, it would be wise to sketch briefly the "son of man" figure in the immediate and broad context of Daniel 7. Daniel 7 is one of the most complex and difficult passages in all of Scripture, and there's little agreement among scholars. Key to understanding nearly all of the book of Daniel is to grasp the flow of Daniel 2. According to Daniel 2, four kingdoms (i.e, Babylon, Medo-Persia, Greece, and Rome) consecutively emerge, but the fourth and final kingdom gives way to God's eternal kingdom. The "stone," symbolizing either the coming Messiah or the eternal kingdom, crushes the four pagan kingdoms (Dan. 2:44–45). The visionary material in Daniel 7–12 rehearses the *same* eschatological drama but

---

3   This section on Daniel is drawn from Benjamin L. Gladd, "An Apocalyptic Trinitarian Model: The Book of Daniel's Influence on Revelation's Conception of the Trinity," in *The Essential Trinity: New Testament Foundations and Practical Relevance*, ed. Brandon D. Crowe and Carl R. Trueman (Phillipsburg, NJ: P&R, 2017), 169–72. Used by permission of P&R Publishing.

with more precision. We learn more about the stone and more about the inner workings of the four kingdoms.

In Daniel 7, the Ancient of Days (Dan. 7:9) judges the earthly pagan kingdoms and establishes his eternal kingdom through the ministry of the "son of man" (7:13). A central difference between Daniel 2 and Daniel 7–12 lies in the finer details of how the four kingdoms interact with one another and how, through the "son of man," God's kingdom will vanquish the previous pagan kingdoms. We should identify the four beasts in Daniel 7 with the four parts of the statue in Daniel 2. The beasts "were stirring up the great sea" (Dan. 7:2). The sea symbolizes chaos, evil, and rebellion. These kingdoms are grotesque, representing their arrogance and destructive nature.

The vision then reverts to the heavenly throne, where a mysterious figure, "one like a son of man," travels on the clouds to the Ancient of Days (Dan. 7:13). The son of man then receives a reward:

> And to him was given dominion
> and glory and a kingdom,
> that all peoples, nations, and languages
> should serve him;
> his dominion is an everlasting dominion,
> which shall not pass away,
> and his kingdom one
> that shall not be destroyed. (Dan. 7:14)

The second half of the chapter (Dan. 7:15–27) interprets the initial vision (7:2–14). The four beasts symbolize four kings or kingdoms (Dan. 7:17). The final kingdom is discussed in some detail, particularly the little horn (Dan. 7:8). The "ten horns" refer to ten kings (Dan. 7:24). This final horn or king antagonizes other kings, persecutes and deceives the Israelites, and speaks against God (Dan. 7:20–21, 24–25).

Identifying the "son of man" figure with precision is notoriously difficult. The language of 7:13–14 does not easily yield itself to interpreters. In the book of Daniel, the phrase "son of man" or "sons of men" is a general reference to humanity (e.g., Dan. 2:38; 5:21). The Greek translations of Daniel (LXX-Theo and OG) use the phrase as a reference to humanity (Dan. 2:38), priests (3:84), Daniel himself (8:17), and angels (10:16). Thus, the phrase falls into two general categories: human and angelic.

Giving us deeper insight into the character is the way in which the "son of man" appears. Critically, the son of man rides on the clouds: "*with the clouds of heaven* there came one like a son of man" (Dan. 7:13). In the Old Testament, riding on the clouds is reserved for God alone (e.g., Ex. 19:9; Pss. 18:11; 97:2; 104:3; Ezek. 1:4). Even angels are not privileged to do so. Therefore, *the book of Daniel symbolically casts the son of man as an enigmatic, divine figure.*[4] How this figure relates to the Ancient of Days is unclear in the immediate context. One hint occurs in Daniel 7:13: "he [the son of man] came to the Ancient of Days." At the very least, the son of man enjoys a unique relationship to the Ancient of Days.[5]

But that is not all. Perhaps the reason the heavenly figure is described as a "son of man" stems from the close identification with a remnant of righteous Israelites. For example, the son of man receives "dominion

---

4   The LXX (OG) of Dan. 7:13 confirms that the son of man has divine qualities: "I saw in a vision at night, and, look, *as* [*hōs*] a son of man came on the heavenly clouds, and *as* [*hōs*] the Ancient of Days he was present, and the attendants were present *with him* [*autō* (this figure); my trans.]." According to Dan. 7:9, the Ancient of Days takes his seat on the throne. A few verses later, in Dan. 7:13, the prophet sees another figure described "as" or "like" the son of man. Is this figure angelic? Possibly, but the remainder of the verse answers in the negative, for the son of man bears the title "like the Ancient of Days." Seyoon Kim rightly puts the pieces together: "We must conclude that the heavenly figure 'like a son of man' is described also as having been 'like the Ancient of Days.' . . . That is, Daniel saw, besides the Ancient of Days, a heavenly figure 'like a son of man and like the Ancient of Days'" (*The 'Son of Man' as the Son of God*, WUNT 30 (Tübingen: Mohr Siebeck, 1983], 23). The OG appears to interpret the son of man as a divine figure. In addition, the identification of *autō* in Dan. 7:13 with son of man furthers this interpretation in that the LXX sees angels ministering or worshiping *him*, the son of man.

5   One early text presents a "son of man" figure as preexistent: "he [the son of man] was concealed in the presence of (the Lord of the Spirits) prior to the creation of the world, and for eternity" (1 En. 48.6). This text and others like it (e.g., 1 En. 62.7–9) cast this son of man figure as existing before creation. For further discussion of how Judaism in general and early Christianity developed a preexistent notion of the coming end-time ruler or Messiah, see Simon J. Gathercole, *The Preexistent Son: Recovering the Christologies of Matthew, Mark, and Luke* (Grand Rapids, MI: Eerdmans, 2006).

and glory and a kingdom" (Dan. 7:14). Later, in the interpretative portion of the vision, the remnant or the "saints of the Most High" replace the son of man and "receive the kingdom and possess the kingdom forever" (Dan. 7:18; see 7:22, 27). The son of man is functionally identified with the saints.

In the Old Testament, kings often embody the nation (e.g., 2 Sam. 21:1; 1 Chron. 21:1–17), so in Daniel 7 the son of man represents the righteous Israelites (hence the phrase "son of *man*"). When he conquers the fourth and final beast, his actions are thus transferred to the group. The remnant inherits the kingdom, since the son of man, their representative, has vanquished their enemy. Conversely, what is true of the righteous Israelites is also true of the son of man. Daniel 7:21 reads, for example, "This horn made war with the saints and prevailed over them." Here the remnant endures severe persecution, intimating that the son of man, too, will suffer intensely. A handful of scholars even connect Daniel's son of man to Adam in Genesis 1–3. Conceptually, it makes good sense, as Daniel 7 portrays the son of man subduing four beasts.[6]

To summarize, the general thrust of Daniel 7 is the end-time judgment of the Ancient of Days on pagan kingdoms and the establishment of his eternal kingdom through the ministry of the son of man. Although these rebellious kingdoms persecute God's people, perhaps even the son of man, God will deliver them and install his kingdom. The son of man's relationship to the Ancient of Days is unresolved, and it's unclear *how* the son of man will conquer the four kingdoms (through suffering?). What's clear, though, is that the son of man will emerge victorious and that the saints will inherit the eternal kingdom.

The Temptation and the Beginning of the Son of Man's Cosmic Rule (4:1–13)

On the surface, the wilderness temptation may seem like an odd place to start in carving out a theology of the Son of Man in Luke's narrative.

---

6 See G. K. Beale, *A New Testament Biblical Theology: The Unfolding of the Old Testament in the New* (Grand Rapids, MI: Baker Academic, 2011), 83–84.

After all, the first occurrence of "Son of Man" lies in Luke 5:24. Commentators rightly draw lines of correspondence between Jesus and Israel in the wilderness temptation, but the verbal exchange between Jesus and the devil reveals an important and often-neglected layer.

Matthew and Mark narrate the wilderness temptation following Jesus's baptism (Matt. 3:13–4:11; Mark 1:9–13), whereas Luke prefaces the temptation with a genealogy (Luke 3:23–38). The last two lines of the genealogy read, "the son of Adam, the son of God" (3:38). What's the significance? Why trace Jesus's ancestry back to humanity's progenitor? Luke wants his readers to view the wilderness temptation through the lens of Adam. Jesus is the second Adam who has come to do what Adam, Noah, Abraham, and Israel failed to do—that is, perfectly trust God's promises, subdue evil, and ensure that God's glorious presence reaches the far corners of the earth. Adam's failure in the garden and Israel's failure in the wilderness wanderings set the stage for Jesus's success in the wilderness temptation (see chapter 5).

The devil appears to tempt Jesus at the end of a forty-day fast in the Judean wilderness, perhaps when he is most vulnerable (Luke 4:2; cf. Matt. 4:2). While all three temptations are important, we need only survey the second and third. The devil leads Jesus to a "high place" where they could view "all the kingdoms of the world" (Luke 4:5 NIV). While we are not privy to the precise mechanics of the vision, a major point of the second temptation is that the devil claims to possess "authority" over the earthly kingdoms and promises to hand over these kingdoms to Jesus if he will "worship" him (4:6–7).

The devil's promise in the second temptation is remarkably similar to the LXX (OG) of Daniel 7:14 (see table 6.1).[7]

---

7   François Bovon mentions that Luke 4:6 is "reminiscent" of Dan. 7:14 and that it is a "linguistic parody" (*Luke 1: A Commentary on the Gospel of Luke 1:1–9:50*, Hermeneia, trans. Christine M. Thomas [Minneapolis: Fortress, 2002], 143). While he rightly notices the connection between Luke 4:6 and Dan. 7:14, he fails to tease out its significance in the immediate context of Luke's narrative.

Table 6.1   Comparison of Daniel 7:14 and Luke 4:6

Daniel 7:14 (NETS translation of LXX-OG)	Luke 4:6
"And royal *authority* [*exousia*] *was given* [*edothē*] to him, and all the nations of the earth according to posterity, and all *honor* [*doxa*] was serving him. And his *authority* [*exousia*] is an everlasting *authority* [*exousia*]."	"To you *I will give* [*dōsō*] all this *authority* [*tēn exousian*] and their *glory* [*tēn doxan*]."

If the allusion is valid, *then the devil may be consciously parodying the Ancient of Days in the prophecy of Daniel 7.* Commentators neglect the implications of this allusion and the wider context of Daniel 7, so we will attempt to understand the wilderness temptation against the backdrop of Daniel 7.

The Ancient of Days appears to "give" the eternal kingdom to the son of man on account of his successful defeat of the fourth beast (Dan. 7:14; see 7:11). Pushing deeper into Daniel 7, we notice that boastful words spew from the little horn or ruler of the fourth beast (Dan. 7:8, 11). Later, in the interpretative portion of the chapter, the little horn "shall speak words against the Most High . . . and shall think to change the times and the law" (Dan. 7:25). Furthermore, Daniel 11:36 states that he "shall exalt himself and magnify himself above every god, and shall speak astonishing things against the God of gods." When we compare Daniel 7 and Luke 4, a handful of connections jump out at us in astonishing ways.

First, the Ancient of Days alone possesses the authority to hand over the kingdom to the Son of Man—not the devil (Dan. 7:9–10). As a result of Adam and Eve's fall, God, in his wisdom and sovereignty, *temporarily* handed over the earthly domain to the devil (see e.g., Job 1:6–12; 2:17; Rev. 12:7–12). The devil's statement that his authority "has been given" (*paradedotai*; NIV) to him is correct.[8] Elsewhere in

---

8   The passive form of *didōmi* is nearly a technical term in Revelation and may even be derived from Dan. 7:14 when dominion "is given" (*edothē*) to the son of man. Throughout the book of Revelation, God or the Lamb issues decrees that Satan/demons execute (see e.g., Rev. 7:2; 8:3; 9:1, 3, 5; 13:5, 7, 14–15). For example, in 6:2 the Lamb gives a demonic agent (the white horse) the authority to wage warfare on the church and unbelievers. Additionally, in

the Synoptics, the devil is labeled the "prince of the demons" (Matt. 9:34; 12:24; Mark 3:22; Luke 11:15). According to John 12:31, he is the "ruler of this world" (cf. John 14:30; 16:11; cf. 1 John 5:19). Paul even calls him the "god of this world" (2 Cor. 4:4) and the "prince of the power of the air" (Eph. 2:2; cf. Mart. Isa. 2:4; CD 5.18; 1QM 17.5). The New Testament affirms that the devil was indeed given the right to rule over the earth for a discrete amount of time, but he was never given the authority to hand it over.[9]

Second, a chief characteristic of the little horn is his boastful and blasphemous speech. Could it be that the devil's blasphemous promise that he has the authority to hand over the kingdom in Luke 4 unwittingly fulfills the prophecy of the little horn in Daniel 7 and 11? Probably. To tempt Jesus, Satan appears to invoke the prophecy of Daniel 7:13–14 *by assuming his role as Ancient of Days.* But his temptation is also blasphemous—thereby fulfilling Daniel 7:8, 25; 11:36. This line of temptation is not a far cry from the serpent's promise in the garden where he audaciously manipulates God's law (Gen. 3:1, 4–5). Recall that the devil even "disguises himself as an angel of light" (2 Cor. 11:14), who often imitates God in assaulting the covenant community (see also Rev. 6:2). At the wilderness temptation, then, Satan once again cloaks himself in divine garb and attempts to deceive not just the children of God but *the* Son of God. Ever since the garden, humanity has succumbed to Satan's lies and deceit, but here in the wilderness temptation he will not succeed.

Third, the son of man's success in Daniel 7 earns him the right to possess all dominion. The book of Daniel *may* have in mind the son of man's authority not only over physical rulers but also spiritual rulers. According to Daniel 10, the angel Gabriel informs Daniel that the "prince of the kingdom of Persia" fought against the archangel Michael (Dan. 10:13). A few verses later, Gabriel goes on to state that he will

---

Rev. 12:3, Satan (the red dragon) possesses ten horns and seven crowns—a clear sign of his authority to rule over the spiritual and physical domains.

9   In commending on Luke 4:6, Robert Stein agrees: "God has placed this world's kingdoms under the devil's temporary rule. God is clearly sovereign, but within his permissive will the devil is temporarily given this authority. This statement explains why the next one is true" (*Luke*, NAC [Nashville: Broadman, 1992], 147).

"fight against *the prince* [*archontos* (LXX-Theo)] of Persia" and that the "*prince* [*ho archōn* (LXX-Theo)] of Greece will come" (Dan. 10:20). These spiritual or heavenly "princes" (*hai archai*) appear to possess some authority over their corresponding earthly kingdoms (Persia and Greece). Daniel 7:14 in the Theodotion recension states, "And to him [the son of man] was given *the dominion* [*hē archē*] and the honor and the kingship" (NETS). The point is that perhaps the son of man's authority extends beyond the earthly kingdom reaching into the spiritual realm.[10] The physical and the spiritual kingdoms are inseparable.

While it may appear that I am leaning too hard on Daniel 7 and grasping at intertextual straws, Jesus's ministry in Luke (and the other three Gospels) makes good sense in light of these connections. While Daniel 7 is certainly one of the most difficult passages in all of Scripture, there's little doubt that the passage is absolutely formative to the Evangelists' depiction of Jesus in the Gospels. Daniel 7 must be understood in light of the book of Daniel as a whole. *If* Daniel 7 informs Luke's account of the wilderness temptation, then we must grapple with his larger point: Jesus's success against the wiles of the devil earns him the right to rule over earthly and spiritual realities. Such a suggestion makes wonderful sense as we move forward in Luke's narrative, as Jesus relentlessly casts out demons and affirms his Danielic "authority" over them (Luke 4:31–37, 41; 8:26–39; 9:1).

The Transfiguration and the Son of Man as the Ancient of Days (9:28–36)

The transfiguration, an event that all three Synoptics record (Matt. 17:1–8; Mark 9:2–8; Luke 9:28–36), continues to narrate Jesus's rule as the Son of Man. While many commentators tend to read the transfiguration in isolation, untethered from Jesus's faithfulness in the wilderness temptation, we must read the two events together. The transfiguration adds yet another layer to his identity as the Son of Man. In Luke 4, the

---

10 See the discussion in G. K. Beale and Benjamin L. Gladd, *Hidden But Now Revealed: A Biblical Theology of Mystery* (Downers Grove, IL: IVP Academic, 2014), 154.

Ancient of Days crowns Jesus as cosmic king and ruler over the cosmos on account of his faithfulness. As we will see, Jesus pulls the curtain back and reveals his divinity.

Luke prefaces this event with the temporal expression "about eight days" (Luke 9:28), an expression that glues the transfiguration to the end of Jesus's passion prediction in the previous passage (9:21–27). At the end of that section, Jesus claims that he, the Son of Man, will come "in his glory and the glory of the Father and of the holy angels" (Luke 9:26) and that some of his disciples will see "the kingdom of God" (9:27). The apocalyptic terms—"Son of Man," "glory," and "kingdom of God"—allude to Daniel 7:13–14.[11] While Jesus's prediction is laced with enigma, the transfiguration presages his arrival as Daniel's Son of Man to judge wickedness and vindicate his true disciples.

Peter, James, and John are the only disciples to experience the transfiguration firsthand, as only they are privy to special revelatory events (cf. Luke 8:51). Luke describes Jesus's face as being "altered" and his clothes becoming "dazzling white" (9:29; cf. Matt. 17:2; Mark 9:2). The Evangelists rarely mention Jesus's attire (cf. John 19:23), so Luke's audience is expected to ponder its significance. Why mention his clothing at this juncture? We noted above that Jesus alludes to Daniel 7 a few verses earlier in Luke 9:26–27, inviting his disciples to view the transfiguration in light of this passage. If we are right to put our finger on Daniel 7, we may have yet another point of contact with that Old Testament passage.

One of the most graphic descriptions in Daniel 7 is that of the Ancient of Days:

As I looked,

> thrones were placed,
>> and the Ancient of Days took his seat;
> his clothing was white as snow,

---

11   David W. Pao and Eckhard J. Schnabel, "Luke," in *Commentary on the New Testament Use of the Old Testament*, ed. G. K. Beale and D. A. Carson (Grand Rapids, MI: Baker Academic, 2007), 311.

> and the hair of his head like pure wool;
>> his throne was fiery flames;
>>> its wheels were burning fire. (Dan. 7:9)

Luke takes a divine symbol from Daniel 7 and places it squarely on Jesus at the transfiguration, affirming that Jesus is fully divine. Though white clothing refers to angelic messengers in the Old Testament and Judaism (e.g., Dan. 12:6; 1 En. 71:1; 2 En. 37:1; cf. Matt. 28:3; Mark 16:5; John 20:12) and recalls the high priest's attire on the Day of Atonement (Lev. 16:3–4), Jesus's appearance exceeds that of the angels. Clearly, the dominant Old Testament background is Exodus 33, where Moses desires to see God's "glory" (Ex. 33:18). But God forbids it, because Moses "cannot see [his] face . . . and live" (Ex. 33:20). Instead, Moses only catches a glimpse of God's "back" (Ex. 33:23). What Moses wished for, the three disciples experience in Luke 9. The God of Sinai is the God of the transfiguration.

While the book of Exodus is key to unlocking the transfiguration, we must not discount the importance of Daniel 7 and the emphasis on Jesus's luminescent clothing.[12] The Son of Man appears to participate in the divine attributes of the Ancient of Days, as clothing in the Old Testament symbolizes inheritance rights and one's right to rule. When biblical authors mention God's garments (e.g., Isa. 6:1), they underscore his unique prerogative to rule over all of creation.[13] God has no rival. So when Jesus appears with divine garb at the transfiguration, *he's identifying himself as the Son of Man from Daniel 7 and affirming his cosmic rule alongside the Ancient of Days.* What is true of the Father,

---

12 Pao and Schnabel suggest that the "cloud" in 9:34 has points of contact with "God's eschatological presence" in texts such as Ezek. 10:3–4 and Dan. 7:13–14 ("Luke," 311). While it's possible that the imagery of a cloud recalls Dan. 7, the strongest link to Dan. 7 is through the title "Son of Man" in Luke 9:26 and 9:44 and in the language of "glory" and "angels" in 9:26.

13 Shawn W. Flynn, "YHWH's Clothing, Kingship, and Power: Origins and Vestiges in Comparative Ancient Near Eastern Contexts," in *Dress and Clothing in the Hebrew Bible: "For All Her Household Are Clothed in Crimson,"* ed. Antonios Finitsis, LHBOTS 679 (London: T&T Clark, 2019), 28.

the Ancient of Days, is also true of Christ, the Son of Man. In the in-augural vision of the book of Revelation, John sees that "the hairs of his [Son of Man's] head were white, like white wool, like snow" (Rev. 1:14). According to Daniel 7:9, the Ancient of Days has "hair . . . like pure wool," probably symbolizing wisdom and purity. Like Luke, John takes a divine symbol that is reserved for God alone and unflinchingly places it on the Son of Man.

At the transfiguration, then, the Father affirms the Son's cosmic rule and recommissions him in the same breath: "This is my Son, my Chosen One; listen to him!" (Luke 9:35).[14] Christ's rule over the cosmos that began at the wilderness temptation continues even in the face of grave suffering that lies ahead (Luke 9:22, 44). Peter, James, and John must remain convinced that Jesus is who he claims to be and that his eternal kingdom will overthrow all forms of rebellion.

Passion Week and the Opposition of the Jewish Leaders (20:1–2)

At the end of Luke's presentation of the wilderness temptation, the Evangelist remarks, "And when the devil had ended every temptation, he departed from him *until an opportune time*" (Luke 4:13). Interpret-ers have speculated about what Luke means by "an opportune time." Is this a reference to Judas's betrayal, the cross, or other events? Key to unlocking this poignant expression is to grasp the devil's relationship with demons *and* false teachers.

Demons don't act alone. Satan, the captain, organizes and directs the fallen angels. We mentioned above that all three Synoptics label him the "prince of demons" (Matt. 9:34; 12:24; Mark 3:22; Luke 11:15). So when we come across any form of demonic activity in Jesus's ministry, we must assume that the devil stands behind it. But if Jesus has conquered Satan in the wilderness temptation, then why does the devil remain active? Jesus's victory, while decisive, was only an initial defeat of the devil. His grasp on this world was broken, but

---

14 See also 3:22, where Jesus fulfills messianic and prophetic expectations of Deut. 18:15, 2 Sam. 7, and Isa. 42:1.

he continues to influence and inspire. Jesus's interactions with the demons can, therefore, be understood as "mopping-up operations."[15] But wasn't the decisive victory won at the cross and resurrection, not at the temptation? An additional layer of demonic activity persists: the onslaught of false teaching. The devil not only orders the demons to do his bidding but also inspires false teachers to wage war against the covenant community through lies and deceit. The New Testament presents an interesting chain of command in this regard:

The devil

↓

The antichrist

↓

False teachers

The devil stands behind the antichrist, and the antichrist stands behind false teachers (see Rev. 13:11–17). Paul says, for example, that "the mystery of lawlessness is already at work" in the false teachers within the church (2 Thess. 2:7). And John adds, "It is the last hour, and as you have heard that antichrist is coming, so now many antichrists have come" (1 John 2:18). While the antichrist has yet to appear physically, he inspires false teachers to speak on his behalf.

Returning to the Third Gospel, we can better discern this theme in Luke's narrative. Immediately following the triumphal entry (Luke 19:28–44), Jesus comes to the temple where he "began to *drive out* [*ekballein*] those who sold" (19:45). Jesus's actions in the temple should not be underestimated, as they occupy in many ways a climactic point of Jesus's earthly ministry. Instead of the temple functioning as a "house of prayer" (19:46, quoting Isa. 56:7) that welcomes the nations into

15 Beale, *New Testament Biblical Theology*, 220.

the presence of God, the nation of Israel transformed it into a "den of robbers" (19:46, alluding to Jer. 7:11). All three Synoptics employ the verb "drive out" (*ekballō*) in describing this event, and all three often use this identical word to narrate the exorcisms. For example, in Luke 9:49 the disciple John remarks, "Master, we saw someone *casting out* [*ekballonta*] demons in your name."[16] Perhaps Luke wants his audience to view Jesus's "driving out" the money changers on a physical and spiritual plane. Jesus not only judges earthly authorities but also spiritual authorities as the successful Son of Man. The physical and the spiritual dimensions are fused together. This line of thinking anticipates the following clash in Luke 20.

At the beginning of Luke 20, the Jewish authorities are steeled in their resolve to kill Jesus (19:47), so they ask him while assembled at the temple, "Tell us by what authority you do these things, or who it is that gave you this authority [to judge the temple]" (20:2). The words "give" and "authority" take on prominence in the Third Gospel:

> And [he] said to him, "To you *I will give* [*dōsō*] all this *authority* [*tēn exousian*] and their glory; for *it has been delivered* [*paradedotai*] to me, and *I give* [*didōmi*] it to whom I will." (4:6)

> And he called the twelve together and *gave* [*edōken*] them power and *authority* [*exousian*] over all demons and to cure diseases. (9:1)

> Behold, *I have given* [*dedōka*] you *authority* [*tēn exousian*] to tread on serpents and scorpions, and over all the power of the enemy, and nothing shall hurt you. (10:19)

Remarkably, the pairing of these two words, "giving" and "authority," exclusively occurs in the context of demonic activity. The majority of the Jewish authorities are, probably unconsciously, taking on the char-

---

16 See also, e.g., Matt. 7:22; 8:16, 31; 9:33; Mark 1:39; 3:15, 22; 6:13; 7:26; Luke 9:40; 11:14–15, 18–20; 13:32.

acteristics of their leader—the devil. Though defeated, Satan continues to set himself against Jesus's ministry by inspiring these Jewish leaders. According to 4:6, the devil parodies the Ancient of Days by promising to "give" the "authority" of the kingdoms to the Son of Man through false worship. Because Jesus resists the temptation, the Ancient of Days "gives" the Son of Man the "authority" over the kingdoms. When the Jewish leaders ask, "Tell us by what *authority* you do these things, or who it is that *gave* you this authority," Luke's careful readers know the answer—the Ancient of Days.[17]

The Son of Man Seated at the Father's Right Hand (22:66–71)

According to all four Gospels, Jesus endures a total of four trials at the end of Passion Week—three Jewish trials (one unofficial trial and two official trials) and one Roman trial. Immediately following Jesus's arrest, John records an unofficial Jewish trial at the palace of Annas (John 18:13–24). Matthew and Mark then mention a second trial later on Thursday night before the Sanhedrin at the residence of Annas or Caiaphas (Matt. 26:59–66; Mark 14:55–64). Luke is the only Evangelist to record a third Jewish trial taking place early Friday morning before the Sanhedrin in the chamber of the Jerusalem temple (Luke 22:66–71). The Sanhedrin found Jesus guilty of blasphemy in their initial examination a few hours before (Matt. 26:66; Mark 14:64), so now the council attempts to charge him officially and hand him over to Pilate.

The exchange between Jesus and the Jewish leaders in Luke 22:66–71 is exceedingly dense, so we will focus only on a single thread. The Sanhedrin asks Jesus, "If you are the Christ, tell us" (22:67). In the first trial before the Sanhedrin, the religious authorities asked him this precise question, to which Jesus replied "I am" (Mark 14:62; cf. Matt. 26:64). But this time around, Jesus refuses to answer the same question directly. After he tells them that they are unable to grasp his identity

---

17 Joel B. Green states, "Luke's audience knows already of Jesus' authority," but Green doesn't tie it to Jesus's identity as the successful Son of Man (*The Gospel of Luke*, NICNT [Grand Rapids, MI: Eerdmans, 1997], 700).

fully (Luke 22:67–68), Jesus says, "*From now on* [*apo tou nyn*] the Son of Man shall be seated at the right hand of the power of God" (22:69).

Jesus fuses two critical Old Testament texts here: Daniel 7:13–14 and Psalm 110:1. While the Jewish authorities inquire into his identity as Israel's King so that they might charge him with treason against the Roman Empire, Jesus affirms his identity as Israel's Messiah *and* her divine, preexistent Lord. Furthermore, the temporal phrase "from now on" (*apo tou nyn*) occurs six times in Luke-Acts, wherein it almost always refers to significant redemptive-historical transitions (see Luke 1:48; 5:10; 12:52; 22:18; Acts 18:6; cf. Matt. 26:64). Jesus claims that his imminent death, resurrection, and ascension will complete his heavenly journey to the Ancient of Days. The journey began at the wilderness temptation with the Ancient of Days initially handing over the eternal kingdom to Jesus. The Father then affirms Jesus's mission and identity as the Son of Man at the transfiguration. Finally, Jesus knows full well that God will crown him as the exalted Son of Man *after* his death and resurrection at the ascension. His imminent death, only hours away, further qualifies him for his cosmic reign. At the wilderness temptation, Jesus's faithfulness in warding off the devil's deception initially qualified him to ascend to the Ancient of Days. But his atoning work on the cross signals the final death knell of Satan.

The Son of Man, the second Adam, overcomes the failures of the first Adam by means of his active and passive obedience. Whereas the first Adam should have subdued the serpent from the garden by trusting in God's promises,[18] Jesus vanquishes the devil in the wilderness by clinging to his Father's will (active obedience). The second Adam, too, must pay the penalty for the sins of the first Adam (passive obedience). Joel Marcus even argues that the unique wording of the Greek phrase *ho huios tou anthrōpou* means "son of *the* man," ultimately alluding to Adam.[19] Oftentimes, Jesus uses the phrase "Son of Man" in conjunction with suffering (see, e.g., Matt. 8:20; 12:40; 17:12; Mark 8:31; 9:12;

---

18 See discussion in Benjamin L. Gladd, *From Adam and Israel to the Church: A Biblical Theology of the People of God*, ESBT 1 (Downers Grove, IL: IVP Academic, 2019), 22–25.

19 Joel Marcus, "Son of Man as Son of Adam," *RB* 110, no. 1 (2003): 38–61.

10:45; Luke 9:22, 44; John 3:14; 8:28), and it may not be a matter of coincidence that Daniel 7 itself subtly anticipates a suffering son of man figure (Dan. 7:13–14, 21, 25). In sum, the active and passive obedience of Christ, the Son of Man, qualifies him to sit at the Father's right hand as the supreme ruler of the cosmos.

The Ascension of the Son of Man (24:50–53)

At the end of chapter 1, we touched on how Jesus's ascent to the Father's throne is the climax of the Third Gospel and how it connects to the u-shaped pattern of Jesus's ministry. Jesus became low so that he might be high and lifted up. I noted that Luke mentions Jesus's ascension twice, once in Luke 24:51 and again in Acts 1:9, with the latter alluding to Daniel 7:13–14. When the Father receives the Son into heaven, he declares his Son's ministry a success and rewards him as cosmic Lord. The Son of Man has successfully achieved the goal set before him and is now qualified to rule over all creation. The Son of Man's journey to the Ancient of Days is now complete.

But Luke's Gospel doesn't end there. In Luke 24:52–53 we read, "And [the disciples] *worshiped* [*proskynēsantes*] him and returned to Jerusalem with great joy, and were continually in the temple blessing God" (cf. Matt. 28:17). The term *proskyneō* ("worship") occurs with frequency (some twenty-nine times) in the Gospels, especially in Matthew. Luke, though, limits this term to two occasions: the wilderness temptation (Luke 4:7–8) and the ascension (24:52). Its use in the temptation narrative brings us full circle to the beginning of the Son of Man's rule. Notice how proper worship is tethered to Daniel 7:

and [the devil] said to [Jesus], "To you I will give all this authority and their glory, for it has been delivered to me, and I give it to whom I will [alluding to Dan. 7:14]. If you, then, *will worship* [*proskynēsēs*] me, it will all be yours." And Jesus answered him, "It is written

"'You *shall worship* [*proskynēseis*] the Lord your God,
and him only shall you serve.'" (Luke 4:6–8)

The devil tempts Jesus to break fellowship with and dependence on his Father by worshiping him. Jesus parries the attack with a quotation of Deuteronomy 6:13, affirming that worship is reserved for God alone. So when the disciples worship Jesus at the end of the Third Gospel, they celebrate Jesus as the enthroned, divine Son of Man.[20]

The Coming the Son of Man (21:25–36)

Our final analysis concerns the return of the Son of Man in judgment in AD 70, an event prophesied in the Olivet Discourse (see Matt. 24:1–25:46; Mark 13:1–37; Luke 21:5–36). I discuss this event last, as it predicts Jesus's activity after his ascension. In Luke 21:7, the disciples ask Jesus two questions: "Teacher, when will these things [the destruction of the temple] be, and what will be the sign when these things are about to take place?" (21:7). Mark and Luke's accounts agree with one another in that they appear to ask the *same* question from two different perspectives (Mark 13:4; Luke 21:7). The first question relates to the general timing of the temple's destruction, whereas the second concerns a "sign" that signals its precise arrival. Matthew's account, though, includes two distinct questions. According to Matthew 24:3, the disciples' first question relates to the timing of the temple's destruction, whereas their second concerns the "sign" of Jesus's second coming at the end of history. In other words, the judgment of the temple is a different event from the judgment of the cosmos.

Luke's account of the Olivet Discourse follows the broad outline of the other two Evangelists (see table 6.2):

---

20 Alan J. Thompson, *Luke*, EGGNT (Nashville: B&H Academic, 2016), 380, even suggests a chiasm, reinforcing Jesus's divinity:

> *Kai autoi proskynēsantes auton*
>   *hypestrepsan eis Ierousalēm meta charas megalēs*
>   *kai ēsan dia pantos en tō hierō*
> *eulogountes ton theon*

Table 6.2 The Olivet Discourse in Luke

Luke 21:8–19	Events leading to the destruction of the temple in AD 70
Luke 21:25–36	The arrival of the Son of Man

Matthew and Mark include a discrete section that concerns the second coming of Jesus. Both Evangelists preface that section with a similar comment: "But concerning that day [the second coming] or that hour, no one knows, not even the angels in heaven, nor the Son, but only the Father" (Mark 13:32; cf. Matt. 24:36). That critical temporal mark signals a break between the events predicting the destruction of the temple in AD 70 (Matt. 24:15–35; Mark 13:14–30) and the second coming of Jesus at the end of history (Matt. 24:36–25:46; Mark 13:32–36). While Luke commentators tend to interpret 21:25–36 as a reference to the second coming, a good case can be made that it exclusively refers to the destruction of the temple. Since Luke's account includes no such transition, he may be primarily concerned with the destruction of the temple in AD 70 in his use of the Olivet Discourse. However, God's judgment on Israel in AD 70 serves as a prophetic pattern of God's future judgment on unbelievers at the end of history. What takes place in AD 70 will be repeated at the consummation of the age.

Much of the Olivet Discourse concerns general events preceding the destruction of Israel's temple: false teaching (21:8–9), political instability (21:9–10), and persecution (21:12–19). It's not until 21:20 when the reader discovers a concrete signal, pointing to imminent destruction: "when you see Jerusalem surrounded by armies, then know that its desolation has come near" (cf. Dan. 9:27; 11:31; 12:11). A handful of verses later, Luke graphically describes the destruction of the temple using extensive cosmic phenomena (italicized below) in conjunction with a quotation from Daniel 7:13 (in Luke 21:27):

And there will be signs in *sun and moon and stars*, and on the earth distress of nations in perplexity because of the roaring of the sea and the waves, people fainting with fear and with foreboding of what is coming on the world. For the *powers of the heavens will be shaken.* And then they will see the Son of Man coming in a cloud with power and great glory. (Luke 21:25–27)

What takes place on earth reverberates in the heavens. Often in apocalyptic literature, stars symbolize angels, and these angelic figures in turn represent people groups or nations on the earth (see discussion in chapter 2). According to Isaiah 24:19–23, a remarkably similar text, God judges the physical and spiritual dimensions of the cosmos with great finality:

The earth is utterly broken.
. . . .
On that day the LORD will punish
    the host of heaven, in heaven,
    and the kings of the earth, on the earth.
. . . .
Then the *moon* will be confounded
    and the *sun* ashamed,
for the LORD of hosts reigns
    on Mount Zion and in Jerusalem. (Isa. 24:19, 21, 23)

The connections between Isaiah 24:19–23 and Luke 21:25–27 are numerous, but what's of particular interest is the connection between God's judgment on the "host of heaven, in heaven" and the "kings of the earth, on the earth." Elsewhere in the Bible, heavenly luminaries are involved in cosmic warfare (see Judg. 5:20; Dan. 8:10; Rev. 12:4, 7–8). So when the Son of Man spiritually arrives in AD 70, he metes out judgment through the Roman army on the earth. Ironically, the fourth beast in Luke 21 is not the devil or the Romans but the nation of Israel!

The Son of Man's "coming" in Luke 21:27 may also refer to Jesus approaching the Ancient of Days—not necessarily to his arrival to earth. In any case, coinciding with earthly, physical judgment, the Son of Man also judges angels in heaven. This line of thinking coheres well with Luke's emphasis on angelic warfare throughout his narrative (see chapter 2). Consider the following: at the beginning of the narrative, Luke mentions that the angel Gabriel visited Zechariah (1:11–20) and Mary (1:26–38). Why mention the angel's name, for Matthew's Gospel leaves the angel anonymous (Matt. 1:20–25)? The angel Gabriel is explicitly mentioned only two times in Scripture: Daniel 8–9 and Luke 1. In Daniel 8–9, Gabriel interprets Daniel's vision, and while the angel in Daniel 10 is not explicitly identified, he is most likely Gabriel.[21] This connection isn't superfluous, for the angel in Daniel 10 takes on a military role when the "prince of the kingdom of Persia withstood" him (Dan. 10:13). The other archangel, Michael, then steps in to assist Gabriel (Dan. 10:13). The military dimension of angels gains momentum in Luke 2 when, at Jesus's birth, "a multitude of the heavenly host" sings praises to God (Luke 2:13). The phrase "heavenly host" (*stratias ouraniou*) almost certainly refers to an army of angels (for examples of the phrase, see 1 Kings 22:19; 2 Chron. 33:3; Neh. 9:6; Acts 7:42). Our discussion of Jesus's battle with Satan in the wilderness temptation (Luke 4:1–13) and then his declaration in 10:18 that he saw Satan "fall like lightning from heaven" continues to develop this theme.

If we are on the right track, then we must ask why Luke incorporates this theme into his narrative. *Why* does Luke maintain his audience's attention to heavenly warfare? Perhaps for two reasons: (1) It explains the significance of Jesus's identity as the Son of Man. In fulfillment of Daniel 7, Jesus possesses authority over earthly *and* spiritual realities. (2) In light of the Son of Man's success, all of creation is now unified in him, allowing previously estranged people groups to enjoy intimate fellowship with one another.

Conclusion

The Son of Man is Jesus's favorite designation for himself. To outsiders, the title could have meant something like "I," but to those who are

---

21   J. J. Collins, *Daniel*, Hermeneia (Minneapolis: Fortress, 1993), 373.

spiritually attuned the title evokes portions of the Old Testament. Luke employs Daniel 7 at six junctures in his narrative, suggesting that Jesus performs the drama of Daniel 7. At the wilderness temptation, Jesus defeats the devil, the fourth beast, and begins his ascent to the Ancient of Days, where he is crowned with the prerogative to rule over the cosmos. At the transfiguration, Jesus reaffirms his cosmic rule to the disciples and appears in the garb of the Ancient of Days, signifying his identity as the Ancient of Days himself. Then, at his third trial Jesus publicly confesses that his death, resurrection, and ascension will complete his heavenly journey to the Ancient of Days. In AD 70, Jesus, as the Son of Man, metes out judgment on theocratic Israel, also identified as the fourth beast. At the end of Luke's Gospel, Jesus climactically rides on a cloud to the throne of the Ancient of Days, where he sovereignly governs the universe with his Father.

A robust understanding of Jesus's identity as the Son of Man reassures believers that nothing happens outside his control. Christ's rule empowers believers to overcome pain and hardship. His reign also comforts the church because it assures us that wickedness will not go unpunished. The Son of Man executes his right to judge as he sits on his throne. According to Revelation 5, the Son of Man, depicted as a Lamb, opens the "scroll" precisely because he "conquered" evil in his death and resurrection (Rev. 5:5). Contained within this scroll are the subsequent judgments that are unleashed on the devil and the world in the remainder of Revelation.

The Year of Jubilee

FOLLOWING THE TEMPTATION IN THE WILDERNESS, Jesus ventures into the synagogues of Galilee and then to his hometown of Nazareth (Luke 4:16). The first words out of his mouth in 4:18–19 are a quotation of Isaiah 61:1–2. Why does Jesus open his Galilean ministry with this Scripture? Why, too, does he claim, "Today this Scripture has been fulfilled in your hearing" (Luke 4:21)? The challenge of this chapter lies in Luke's deep familiarity with the Old Testament and, especially, the book of Leviticus. To grasp the year of jubilee in Isaiah 61, we must first understand the movement of purification in the Pentateuch. This chapter is a fitting closure of this project on Luke's Gospel because Jesus's recitation of Isaiah 61:1–2 pulls together many of the themes we've covered thus far. God atones for the sins of his people and cleanses his tabernacle *so that* he may dwell with humanity and the created order.

Announcing the Year of Jubilee (4:14–30)

Once Jesus defeats the devil, his first order of business is to turn north and minister in the synagogues of Galilee (4:14–15, 31–33). Matthew and Mark disclose *what* Jesus proclaims: the arrival of the long-awaited kingdom (Matt. 4:17; Mark 1:15). Luke, though, only mentions that Jesus taught in the Galilean synagogues (Luke 4:15). Luke's readers are left wondering what precisely Jesus taught in Galilee.

Luke uniquely places Jesus's rejection in Nazareth at the beginning of his ministry (cf. Matt. 13:53–58; Mark 6:1–6), likely establishing the pattern of Luke-Acts. Jesus's own countrymen reject him in anger, while the Gentiles welcome him with joy. Nazareth, situated on a hill of limestone to the west of the Sea of Galilee, was unremarkable. Some scholars estimate that only about five hundred inhabited the village.[1] Nathanael was not alone when he rhetorically remarked in John 1:46: "Can anything good come out of Nazareth?"

Jesus enters the synagogue on the Sabbath, stands up, and reads from Isaiah 61:1–2. Luke is the only writer to record what Old Testament passage Jesus reads:

He unrolled the scroll and found the place where it was written,

> "The Spirit of the Lord is upon me,
>> because he has anointed me
>> to proclaim good news to the poor.
> He has sent me to proclaim liberty to the captives
>> and recovering of sight to the blind,
>> to set at liberty those who are oppressed,
> to proclaim the year of the Lord's favor." (Luke 4:17–19)

The expressions "liberty to the captives" and "year of the Lord's favor" recall the year of jubilee. Before we delve into the significance of the Isaiah quotation in Luke's Gospel, we first need to grasp the ordinance of the year of jubilee in its original context in Leviticus. The Old Testament background unlocks the meaning of the event in Luke's Gospel, so we need to let the Old Testament set the agenda.

The Prescription of the Year of Jubilee

Leviticus 25:8–55 instructs the Israelites to observe the "year of jubilee" (Lev. 25:13, 28, 40, 50, 52, 54). Every seventh year, the Israelites are to

---

1   Richard A. Freund and Daniel M. Gurtner, "Nazareth," in *T&T Clark Encyclopedia of Second Temple Judaism*, 2 vols., ed. Daniel M. Gurtner and Loren T. Stuckenbruck (New York: T&T Clark, 2020), 2:539.

give the land a Sabbath rest and reap only what grows naturally (Lev. 25:4–7). Then, after the seventh Sabbath rest of the land—that is, after forty-nine years—the Israelites are to announce a year of jubilee (Lev. 25:9–12). Crucially, *the fiftieth year opens with the Day of Atonement, the holiest day of Israel's calendar.* For us to understand the year of jubilee, then, we must turn back a few chapters in Leviticus and consider this incredibly important event.

The Day of Atonement wipes the slate clean, so to speak, allowing unholy Israel to dwell with a holy God (Lev. 16). The critical Hebrew word (*kpr*), often rendered "to atone," conveys two interrelated dimensions in Leviticus and elsewhere: cleansing/purgation and ransom/forgiveness. Sin endangers a person's life, requiring an atoning sacrifice for expiation and forgiveness (e.g., Lev. 17:11), and sin also pollutes God's sanctuary, requiring a cleansing sacrifice (e.g., Lev. 8:15; 16:19).[2] Both ideas, atonement and cleansing, are therefore required to bring God and creation back into harmony.[3]

On the Day of Atonement, the high priest enters the Most Holy Place twice. After sacrificing a bull for a purification offering (atonement for himself and his family), sacrificing a ram as a burnt offering (Lev. 16:3), and bathing and donning white clothes (Lev. 16:4–5), he then enters the Most Holy Place the first time. To protect himself from God's wrath, the high priest must also carry hot coals from the bronze altar in the courtyard and, once inside the Most Holy Place, pour two handfuls of incense over the coals above the mercy seat, creating a cloud that erects a barrier between him and God (Lev. 16:12–13). Then the priest takes the bull's blood and sprinkles it on the lid of the ark and in front of it (Lev. 16:14). The Day of Atonement then progresses into its second stage. Once the high priest makes atonement for himself

---

2   Jay Sklar, "Sin and Impurity: Atoned or Purified? Yes!," in *Perspectives on Purity and Purification in the Bible*, ed. B. J. Schwartz, D. P. Wright, J. Stackert, and S. M. Naphtali (New York: T&T Clark, 2008), 18–31.

3   We should also draw a distinction between "propitiation" and "expiation." Graham Cole puts it well: "An *expiatory* sacrifice is directed towards sin. A *propitiatory* sacrifice is directed towards the wrath of God" (Graham A. Cole, *God the Peacemaker: How Atonement Brings Shalom*, NSBT 25 [Leicester, UK: Apollos, 2009], 143 [italics original]).

and his family (Lev. 16:11–14), he then casts lots over two goats. One goat will be sacrificed, and the other will be released into the wilderness (Lev. 16:8–10). The high priest offers up the designated goat as a purification offering for the nation and sprinkles its blood on and in front of the mercy seat seven times (Lev. 16:15–16). The process appears to be repeated in the Holy Place on the altar of incense (Lev. 16:16) and the outer court (16:20). The high priest, representing the people, places his hands on the scapegoat and then releases it into the wilderness, symbolizing the removal of sin from Israel's camp (16:22).

Three important principles are at work here and resound throughout Scripture:[4] (1) The point of the Day of Atonement is cleansing of sin and uncleanness from the sanctuary and Israel's camp so that God can dwell intimately with his people. Sin distances God and humanity, so atonement is necessary for the two parties to enjoy fellowship. (2) The Day of Atonement is called a "Sabbath of solemn rest" (Lev. 16:31; LXX: *sabbata sabbatōn*). Why? The weekly Sabbath was a sacred event, when God called Israel to enjoy his sanctifying presence (Ex. 31:13). The Day of Atonement, then, brings together two critical elements—space (the sanctuary) and time (the Sabbath)—for drawing near to God. (3) The complex nature of Israel's sacrificial system should be understood as a movement from expiation (purification and reparation offerings—e.g., Lev. 4–5; 16), to consecration (burnt offerings—e.g., Lev. 6:8–13), to fellowship (tribute and peace offerings—e.g., Lev. 7:11–21).[5]

The cultic approach to God also explains the final sacrifice of the liturgy, the peace offering. *The highlight of the peace offering was a communion meal.* Some of the sacrificial meat would be returned to the worshiper who would then enjoy a sacred feast with family and

---

4   This paragraph is conceptually based on L. Michael Morales, *Who Shall Ascend the Mountain of the Lord? A Biblical Theology of the Book of Leviticus*, NSBT 37 (Downers Grove, IL: IVP Academic, 2015), 201.

5   For further discussion of this progression, see L. Michael Morales, *Exodus Old and New: A Biblical Theology of Redemption*, ESBT 2 (Downers Grove, IL: IVP Academic, 2020), 92–98.

friends in the presence of God. Having entered Yahweh's house, one then enjoys his unsurpassed hospitality.[6]

Now that we have surveyed the Day of Atonement in Leviticus 16, we can more fully appreciate the year of jubilee in Leviticus 25. The major principle at work in the prescription of the year of jubilee is that "the land ultimately belongs to God. His people are but *resident aliens and settlers* in the land."[7] Israel recognizes that the promised land is not theirs. They are merely tenants of God's property. The forgiveness of debts and the release of slaves flow from this operating principle. On the basis of the high priest's work on the Day of Atonement (Lev. 25:9), the entire year is deemed "holy." The land must lie fallow (Lev. 25:11–12). The Israelites are to forgive debts, return any land or property procured during the previous forty-nine years (25:13–17, 25–34), help the poor (25:35–38), and release Israelite slaves (25:39–43). All are equal in the sight of God. The cosmos is finally being realigned with Israel's God.[8]

In the year of jubilee, God reminds Israel that they must function as a corporate, faithful Adam who mediates God's rule over the promised land. Adam and Eve, because they were created in God's image, were to represent God on the earth as faithful prophets, priests, and kings. But the first couple failed, so God raised up Israel to represent him to the world as corporate prophets, priests, and kings. If Israel would obey God by fulfilling their covenantal obligations to rule over all forms of rebellion, to embody the divine law, and to mediate God's presence to the nations, then the promise of Leviticus 26:11–12 would come true: "I will make my dwelling among you, and my soul shall not abhor you. And I will walk among you and will be your God, and you shall be my people." This promise is connected to a larger swath of texts that speak to God's ultimate goal in redemption: to dwell consummately

6   Morales, *Exodus Old and New*, 96 (italics mine).
7   Gordon J. Wenham, *The Book of Leviticus*, NICOT (Grand Rapids, MI: Eerdmans, 1979), 320 (italics original).
8   J. B. Green and N. Perrin, "Jubilee," in *Dictionary of Jesus and the Gospels,* 2nd ed, ed. Joel B. Green, Jeannine K. Brown, and Nicholas Perrin (Downers Grove, IL: IVP Academic, 2013), 450.

with humanity and creation in an environment free from the possibility of rebellion, wherein he receives all the glory. While we are unsure whether Israel ever kept the year of jubilee (see Jer. 34:8–16), we can discern traces of it in the historical and prophetic literature (e.g., 2 Kings 19:29–31; Isa. 37:30–32; Ezek. 7:12–13; 11:15).[9] But two Old Testament books in particular tie the year of jubilee to the eschatological restoration of Israel—Isaiah 61 and Daniel 9. Our focus, however, will remain on Isaiah 61, as Jesus himself quotes the passage in Luke 4.

When we compare the year of jubilee in Leviticus 25 with the eschatological year of jubilee in Isaiah 61, we notice several salient developments: (1) The prescriptions of Leviticus 25 morph into a full-blown prophecy in Isaiah 61. Israel fails to keep the year of jubilee, so God promises to ensure its arrival through his anointed servant(s). Isaiah 61, rehearsing a great deal of the restoration prophecies of Isaiah 40–66, announces that Israel's end-time redemption will coincide with the year of jubilee. The messenger or servant heralds "liberty to the captives" and announces the "year of the LORD's favor" (Isa. 61:1–2; cf. Ezek. 46:16–17). (2) The "poor" in Leviticus 25 are largely economically destitute (Lev. 25:25–28, 35–53), whereas the "poor" in Isaiah 61 are primarily spiritually destitute (Isa. 61:1–3). Oswalt rightly draws attention to this development in Isaiah 61:1: The term *poor* "speaks of all who are distressed and in trouble for any reason, including sin."[10] Isaiah 61:1b unpacks what the prophet means by "poor" in 61:1a:

> he has sent me to bind up *the brokenhearted*,
>> to proclaim liberty to *the captives*,
>>> and the opening of the prison to *those who are bound.*

This is none other than a description of the enslaved Israelites in Babylon. It appears, then, that when God redeems his people through

---

9   For a lengthy treatment of the year of jubilee in various Old Testament and Jewish texts, see J. S. Bergsma, *The Jubilee from Leviticus to Qumran: A History of Interpretation* (Leiden: E. J. Brill, 2007).

10   John N. Oswalt, *The Book of Isaiah: Chapters 40–66*, NICOT (Grand Rapids, MI: Eerdmans, 1998), 565.

the ministry of his anointed servant(s) and brings them back into the promised land, an eschatological year of jubilee will mark the occasion. Later in Isaiah 61:6, the prophet divulges the resultant status of these redeemed Israelites:

> but you shall be called the *priests* of the LORD;
>> they shall speak of you as the *ministers* of our God.

The priestly identity of God's people makes beautiful sense in light of our observations of the year of jubilee in Leviticus 25. And while commentators rightly discuss the realization of Israel's mediatorial role in blessing the nations in 61:6 (see Ex. 19:6), another often-unexplored dimension of their priestly role may loom in the background. Recall that the year of jubilee begins with the Day of Atonement (Lev. 25:9), so that the yearlong celebration would be the holiest year of each generation. The whole point of the Day of Atonement and the year of jubilee is to reorient Israel for a proper understanding of their relationship with God and the created order. Israelites must view themselves as a corporate Adam, a corporate priest-king who maintains the sacred space of the temple and mediates God's presence to the nations (see Gen. 2:15). Broadly, the entire book of Isaiah envisions the complete redemption of all things. Heaven and earth will coalesce, and God will fully and finally dwell with his people, ethnic Israelites and Gentiles, in the new Jerusalem or the "new heavens and the new earth" (Isa. 66:22; cf. 65:17). The entire cosmos will, at the end of history, function as God's gigantic Most Holy Place, wherein every member of the redeemed will serve as high priests (Rev. 22:4). All of God's people will stand equal in his sight, minister before him in joy, and cultivate every inch of the rich, new earth. The eschatological year of jubilee is not simply confined to a single year of the calendar but stretches for all of eternity.

Fulfillment of the Year of Jubilee in Luke 4

In light of our Old Testament discussion, we are now is a position to better grasp the significance of Jesus's use of Isaiah 61 in Luke 4:18–19.

Following the quotation, Luke narrates what follows: "And he rolled up the scroll and gave it back to the attendant and sat down. And the eyes of all in the synagogue were fixed on him. And he began to say to them, *'Today this Scripture has been fulfilled in your hearing'*" (4:20–21).

Without a doubt, Jesus identifies himself and his ministry with the anointed servant of Isaiah 61, who announces the end of Israel's exile and the arrival of the new creation. But the fulfillment of the year of jubilee extends beyond merely identifying Jesus with the anointed servant of Isaiah. Significant contact exists between the biblical conception of the year of jubilee and Luke's Gospel at large. Through the ministry of Jesus, creation is now holy, God's people commune with him, and all remain equal in his sight. We will now examine each of these dimensions in turn.

Creation as Holy to the Lord

On the surface, the timing of Jesus's arrival in Nazareth appears most peculiar. After defeating the devil in the Judean wilderness (Luke 4:1–13), why is reading Isaiah 61 Jesus's first order of business? The other two Synoptics place the event later in their narratives (see Matt. 13:53–58; Mark 6:1–6). A robust understanding of the year of jubilee explains the link between the two events. We observed above that the year of jubilee begins with the Day of Atonement (Lev. 25:9). Since the entire year of jubilee is to be consecrated to God (Lev. 25:10), the purging of sin and defilement is necessary. *Perhaps Luke encourages his readers to view, at least partially, the wilderness temptation as the expulsion of the unclean devil from the created order.*[11] Certainly, Christ's atoning death is the fulfillment of the Day of the Atonement in that it deals with sin once and for all, expiating the sins of God's people. One of the most dramatic details of the Day of the Atonement is the expulsion of the live goat bearing Israel's sin from the camp (Lev. 16:8, 10,

---

11   In Luke 2:22, Luke states that Joseph and Mary arrived in Jerusalem "for their purification." This is odd because only the mother is deemed unclean after childbirth (Lev. 12). Perhaps Luke highlights the ritual uncleanness of both parents because of the pervasiveness of the unclean state of Israel and the cosmos.

26). Anything unclean must be driven from the presence of God, who dwells among his people in the Most Holy Place. While Luke doesn't explicitly label the devil "unclean," he twice attributes the adjective "unclean" to demons immediately following his prophetic ministry in Nazareth:

> And in the synagogue there was a man who had the spirit of *an unclean demon* [*daimoniou akathartou*]. (Luke 4:33)

> For with authority and power he commands *the unclean spirits* [*tois akathartois pneumasin*], and they come out! (Luke 4:36)

If demons are unclean, then how much more is their leader, the devil himself?

A dominant pattern in the Pentateuch, especially Leviticus, is the threefold cycle of sin/defilement → purgation/expiation → the preservation of God's glorious presence. Sin must be removed for a holy God to dwell with his people. The problem is, however, that animal sacrifices are unable to remove sin and defilement fully from humanity and the created order.[12] When will the cycle be broken? Jesus's wilderness temptation should be broadly understood against the background of this threefold cycle.

A great deal of Luke 4 concerns the removal of unclean demons from the created order. The general flow of the narrative is as follows:

1. Jesus defeats and expels the devil (4:1–13)
2. The people of Nazareth expel Jesus from their midst (4:14–30)
3. Jesus expels demons in Capernaum (4:31–37)
4. Jesus expels demons at the home of Simon Peter (4:38–41)

---

12 Morales incisively comments on the Day of Atonement: "There must be a Day of Atonement for the cosmos. Ultimately, this annual purgation reiterates the need for a full and final cleansing—one that cannot be threatened or undone—for the covenant promise of humanity's communion and fellowship with God to be realized" (Morales, *Who Shall Ascend?*, 171–72). Since the earthly tabernacle/temple serves as a microcosm of the cosmos, what transpires in the tabernacle/temple must also transpire in the cosmos.

When we take inventory of demonic expulsion in Luke 4, Jesus's ministry in Nazareth becomes all the more glaring. In Nazareth, Jesus's longtime friends and acquaintances "drove him out of the town" (4:29), whereas in Capernaum Jesus expels a multitude of demons (4:35–36, 41). The word "to drive out" (*ekballō*) in 4:29 is used elsewhere in the Third Gospel for the expulsion of demons (9:40, 49; 11:14, 18–20; 13:32). Ironically, Jesus's hometown treats him like a demon in expelling him from their midst! Not coincidentally, Jewish crowds in the Fourth Gospel accuse Jesus on three different occasions of possessing a demon (John 7:20; 8:48; 10:20). This line of thinking may even explain an odd detail in the passage. The crowd takes him to the "brow of *the hill* [*tou orous*] . . . so that they could *throw* him *down* [*katakrēmnisai*] the cliff" (Luke 4:29). Later in Luke 8, pigs grazed on "the hillside" (*tō orei*) and then, possessed by demons, "rushed down *the steep bank* [*tou krēmnou*] into the lake" (8:32–33). Jesus began to expel all unclean things from the cosmos, and he announces the inauguration of the year of jubilee—the arrival of the kingdom and the descent of God's glory. Jesus is not only the herald of Isaiah 61 but also the object of what he proclaims. At the fall, God granted Satan a foothold over the cosmos. Of course, God sovereignly rules over Satan, and Satan cannot thwart God's decrees. At the temptation, Jesus conquers Satan's domain and begins to establish the eternal kingdom. Jesus is now the ruler of the cosmos and realigns it under the reign of God, bringing all of creation into a Sabbath rest.

Communing with a Holy God[13]

One emphasis of Luke's Gospel is Jesus's fellowship with outsiders in the context of meals.[14] And while these meals have received a great deal of scholarly attention in recent years,[15] one glaring omission is connecting them with Israel's sacrificial system, a movement from expiation

---

13 This section excerpted and adapted from pages 233–34, 262–63 of *Handbook on the Gospels* by Benjamin L. Gladd, copyright © 2021. Used by permission of Baker Academic, a division of Baker Publishing Group.

14 See Luke 5:27–32; 7:36–50; 10:38–42; 11:37–54; 14:1–24; 15:1–32; 19:1–10; 24:13–35.

15 For interaction with secondary literature on table fellowship in Luke, see Craig L. Blomberg, *Contagious Holiness: Jesus' Meals with Sinners*, NSBT 19 (Leicester: Apollos, 2005), 130–63.

to consecration to fellowship. Taken together, the aim of the sacrifices is the opportunity for humanity to dwell in the presence of a holy God and participate in a cultic meal. They, in other words, are the *result* of cleansing/expiation and symbolize intimate fellowship with Yahweh.

All three Synoptics follow the basic movement of Jesus ridding the unclean devil from creation (Matt. 4:1–11; Mark 1:11–12; Luke 4:1–13), cleansing humanity from various internal and external effects of sin (Matt. 4:23–25; 8:1–9:8; Mark 1:21–2:12; Luke 4:31–44; 5:12–26), and, finally, eating with humanity in a covenant meal (Matt. 9:9–17; Mark 3:13–17; Luke 5:27–39). *Meals in Luke's Gospel are, then, central to Jesus's ministry in that they indicate his victory over Adam's sin and its effects, and they anticipate the consummate meal in the new Jerusalem when God's people intimately dwell with him* (Rev. 19:17–19).

We will now examine two representative meals in Luke's narrative that embody Jesus's attitude toward sinners and Pharisees. Jesus uses a meal to celebrate the new age and welcome sinners and outsiders (Luke 5:27–32), whereas the Pharisees use meals as an opportunity to pass judgment on Jesus (7:36–50; 11:37–54; 14:1–24).

Luke 5 opens with the calling of Peter, James, and John (Luke 5:1–11) and then progresses to Jesus healing a leper (5:12–16) and a paralyzed man (5:17–26). In the calling of Levi/Matthew in Luke 5:27–32 (// Matt. 9:9–13 // Mark 2:14–17), Luke bundles themes that unfold throughout the Third Gospel.

The first theme involves his description of Levi as a "tax collector" (Luke 5:27). Tax collectors were quite disliked among the populace in the first century, yet they feature prominently in Luke's Gospel (3:12; 7:29, 34; 15:1; 18:10–13). Rome taxed the Jewish people directly and indirectly. On the one hand, Rome used the Jewish leaders to procure tribute directly on their behalf, manifesting itself in a land tax (*tributum soli*) and a head tax (*tributum capitis*); Rome also indirectly outsourced a taxation to a group called tax farmers or "tax collectors."[16] This group

---

16 T. E. Schmidt, "Taxation, Jewish," in *Dictionary of New Testament Background*, ed. Craig A. Evans and Stanley E. Porter (Downers Grove, IL: IVP, 2000), 1165.

collected taxes on goods at ports and tax booths along a road or at the entrance to a city. These tax collectors paid the tribute ahead of time—in full—and then turned around and collected payment as they accosted those passing by. This is how they made their living. Charging exorbitant rates and fees however they deemed fit would not be out of the ordinary. According to early Jewish tradition, tax collectors were associated with thieves and murderers (m. Ned. 3:4). It's not difficult to imagine the disdain all would have for these tax collectors.

Luke mentions that Levi hosts a "great feast" (5:29). The combination of a tax collector (an outsider), a great feast, and "new wine" (5:37–39) evokes Isaiah 25:6 (cf. Gen. 21:8; Rev. 19:9):

> On this mountain the LORD of hosts will make for all peoples
> a feast of rich food, a feast of well-aged wine,
> of rich food full of marrow, of aged wine well refined.

If Isaiah 25 is in view, then Jesus's actions are eschatological. Fulfilling the expectation of Isaiah 25, he is—as Yahweh in the flesh—fellowshiping with all of humanity. Isaiah 25 also mentions that the feast takes place "on this mountain" (Isa. 25:6, 7), a likely reference to the new Jerusalem as the eschatological temple (cf. Isa. 2:2). According to Luke 5, God's glory has arrived in the person of Jesus, and the nations are now enjoying intimate communion with him.

Ironically, those who are hostile to God's work of redemption are not "sinners" (Luke 5:30) but the Jewish leaders—the Bible scholars of the day. Instead of embracing Jesus and his message, the religious authorities are marked with the maxim "the old is good" (5:39). In calling a tax collector and four fishermen to be numbered among the twelve disciples, the nucleus of true Israel, Jesus symbolically announces that the kingdom is largely composed neither of the socially elite nor of the religiously and ritually observant but of ordinary people and the scorned. Furthermore, the law's insistence that a holy God can only dwell in the midst of a holy people is upheld in the person of Jesus who ritually purifies those unclean sinners who trust in him.

Meals take on another layer of significance in the Third Gospel, as Luke records the Pharisees sharing three meals with Jesus (7:36–50; 11:37–54; 14:1–24). The three meals contain a few characteristics (see table 7.1).

Table 7.1 Comparison of Meals Shared by Jesus and Pharisees in Luke

	Evaluation	Issue	Condemnation
Luke 7:36–50	Pharisee "saw" (7:39)	Jesus associating with an unclean sinful woman (7:37–38)	Pharisee lacks love and devotion for Jesus (7:47)
Luke 11:37–54	Pharisee "was astonished to see" (11:38)	Jesus eating with unwashed hands (11:38)	Pharisees lack purity of heart (11:39–41)
Luke 14:1–24	Pharisees "were watching him carefully" (14:1)	Jesus healing on the Sabbath (14:3)	Pharisees lack proper understanding of the Sabbath (14:5) and pursue positions of honor (14:8–14)

Table fellowship is seemingly an odd context for these indictments of the Jewish leaders, since meals symbolize deep friendship and common identity. In all three meals, Pharisees take notice of Jesus's actions. The Pharisees merely observed Jesus in the first two, but during the third and final meal they "were watching him carefully [*ēsan paratēroumenoi auton*]" (14:1). The term "carefully watch" (*paratēreō*) often occurs in the context of individuals spying on someone for the purpose of entrapment (e.g., Dan. 6:12 LXX-Theo; Sus. 12, 15–16). The same term occurs two other times in the Third Gospel, and both concern the religious leaders' desire to trap Jesus (Luke 6:7; 20:20; cf. Mark 3:2; Acts 9:24). Furthermore, all three meals in Luke's narrative follow hostility between Jesus and the Jewish leaders or crowds (Luke 7:30–35; 11:29–32; 13:15–16). Perhaps, then, the religious authorities exploit table fellowship in the third instance as a place for judgment and evaluation. They never intend to enjoy sweet fellowship with Jesus. Much like Haman being hung on his own gallows (Esth. 7:10), the Pharisees use table fellowship as an opportunity to evaluate and condemn Jesus, but he instead evaluates and condemns them!

Equal in the Sight of God

A main, if not *the* main, tenet of the year of jubilee is God's insistence that the Israelites stand on equal footing with one another. According to Leviticus 25:23, the Israelites are deemed "strangers and sojourners" in the land, because the land ultimately belongs to God (cf. 25:35). The Israelites are merely tenants. Furthermore, the Israelites eliminate all debts in the year of jubilee and return one another's property (Lev. 25:25–43). The prophecy of Isaiah 61:1 applies this theme to the exiled Israelites:

> [Yahweh] has sent me [the servant] to bind up *the brokenhearted,*
>> to proclaim liberty to *the captives,*
>> and the opening of the prison to *those who are bound.*

All the captive Israelites, held under the thumb of the mighty Babylonians, are considered spiritually and physically poor and destitute. Only when God restores them in the promised land will they resume their function as God's Adamic tenants in the land.

When we come across the marginalized in the Third Gospel, Luke invites his readers to view each of Jesus's encounters with the poor and outcast as fulfilling Isaiah's prophecy. Notice the reversal of fortunes: Jesus elevates the poor to full-blown tenants of the land—or "priests" and "ministers" (Isa. 61:6)—whereas he disinherits the rich. The poor rule on behalf of God as restored image bearers, but the rich, on account of their idolatry and pride, are denied their tenancy in the land. Once again, Mary's words ring true:

> he has brought down the mighty from their thrones
>> and exalted those of humble estate;
> he has filled the hungry with good things,
>> and the rich he has sent away *empty* [*kenous*]. (Luke 1:52–53)

The word "empty" occurs two other times in Luke's account in the parable of the wicked tenants (20:9–19). When the owner of the vineyard twice sent his servant to the tenants, they persecuted him and both times "sent him away *empty-handed* [*kenon*]" (20:10, 11). On the whole, this parable illustrates the Jewish leaders' failure to obey God's law. God entrusted them, the tenants, with the vineyard (Israel), but they revolted and killed the owner's son so that they might gain the inheritance (20:13–14). Reading the parable of the wicked tenants against the backdrop of the year of jubilee in Leviticus 25 and its eschatological development in Isaiah 61 is striking, and many of the pieces of Luke's narrative fall into place.

As a result of the Jewish leaders' killing the owner's "beloved son" (Luke 20:13), the owner promises to "give the vineyard to others" (20:16). The Lord revokes the Jewish leaders' privilege of leading and guiding the covenant community and hands it over to others. Who are the "others"? They are likely identified as Gentiles and perhaps those within Israel who are weak and marginalized. If the Jewish leaders had obeyed Leviticus 25, they would have understood themselves as humble tenants of the covenant community; instead, they attempted to rule over God's people and assume the position of God himself—the owner. As a result, God promises to "come and destroy those tenants" (Luke 20:16). On the flip side, we should identify all the outsiders within Luke's Gospel with the "strangers and sojourners" of Leviticus 25:23 who wisely manage God's vineyard.

Conclusion

When Jesus reads from Isaiah 61 in the synagogue of his hometown, he discloses the basic outline of his ministry. In fulfillment of Leviticus 25 and Isaiah 61, Jesus atones for the sin of his people, an act that requires assuaging God's wrath and the purification of the cosmos. The wilderness temptation should be partly understood as the expulsion of the unclean devil from the created order. On account of Christ's work, creation is now holy, allowing God's people to intimately commune with him. All redeemed humanity remain equal in his sight. Meals with Jesus of Nazareth in the Third Gospel take on an additional layer of symbolism, too, as they symbolize intimate fellowship with Yahweh. Jesus redeems his people so that they may dwell in the life-giving presence of God.

Looks can be deceiving. It doesn't look like Christ has begun to purify the cosmos and dwell with believers. But, as Paul states, "we walk by faith, not by sight" (2 Cor. 5:7). Believers must recall the precious realities of Christ's work and meditate on them. The arrival of the year of jubilee also affects how we treat one another. Since all believers are equal in the sight of God and have begun to inherit the new creation, we must stamp out anything that inhibits unity among God's people: divisiveness, racism, injustice, and so on. A great deal of the New Testament can be summarized in a handful of words: we must be who we are in Christ.

Epilogue

THE THIRD GOSPEL IS A TREASURE, filled with priceless truths about Christ and what it means to follow him. While I could synthesize dozens of themes, I will only consider three: the certainty of Christ's ministry, the nature of his rule, and our lives in the new creation.

The Certainty of Christ's Ministry

At the outset, Luke discloses to his readers the purpose of his Gospel: "that you [Theophilus] may have certainty concerning the things you have been taught" (Luke 1:4). Theophilus, perhaps a Jewish proselyte who later became a Christian, was probably familiar with Israel's Scriptures and with the broad strokes of Jesus's ministry. So Luke writes his narrative to enrich and affirm Theophilus's understanding of Christ and how such an understanding relates to the Old Testament.

Christians of all ages, especially today, can be confident in what Luke and the other three Evangelists record. Only two of the four Gospels were written by members of the twelve disciples—Matthew and John. Mark and Luke, then, were largely dependent on interviewing the living disciples and gathering firsthand, eyewitness testimony about Jesus's life, death, and resurrection from those who encountered him and knew him personally. Luke's second volume, the book of Acts, narrates the explosion of the gospel throughout the Roman Empire, requiring even more research and investigation. The point is that Luke's Gospel, indeed the whole of the New Testament, rests on the faithful and pristine testimony of the apostles.

We believe precious truths about Jesus *through* the witness of the Old Testament and *through* the witness of the apostles. The Spirit uses both mediums to reveal Christ to believers, impressing on them the trustworthiness of their content. So the more we read the Old Testament and, in our case, the Gospel of Luke, the more our faith and confidence in Christ mature. Christians have always lived in a world of competing truth claims, but due to the plethora of false teaching on the internet and social media, we are far more aware of it than ever before. We are pushed and pulled from every conceivable angle. Believers need to read the Bible more, not less. Only then will we be convinced of the truthfulness of Christ's life and compelled to tell the world about him.

Christ's Rule

In a few chapters, I mapped various threads of the rule of Christ in Luke's Gospel. We learned how Christ rules over his kingdom in an intriguing manner. Christ's success over the devil in the wilderness temptation and his death and resurrection initially establish the end-time kingdom. One kingdom falls and another rises. But Christ's rule and the nature of the kingdom are, from the standpoint of the Old Testament, odd, and his kingdom is unfolding in a rather surprising way. Instead of Christ defeating the Romans and ushering in the kingdom all at once, as the Old Testament generally expected, the kingdom progresses slowly. It begins like a mustard seed, beginning with Jesus, and then the seed germinates, grows through the ministry of the twelve and seventy-two disciples, and, finally, the kingdom extends to the ends of the earth. Luke begins his Gospel with the birth of Christ in the little town of Bethlehem and ends the book of Acts with the apostle Paul "proclaiming the kingdom of God" in the heart of the Roman Empire (Acts 28:31).

There's yet another oddity at work in Christ's kingdom. The kingdom also manifests itself far more spiritually than physically. Yes, the eternal kingdom manifests itself concretely with physical effects, such as the sheer size of the global church and the propagation of the gospel. Nevertheless, earthly rulers still sit on their thrones, often waging war against God's people and fueling injustice. The book of Luke, perhaps more than any other Gospel, articulates the *initial* yet *decisive* fall of Satan's reign and the dissolution of his kingdom. Satan and his minions no longer possess the power over the created order that they once did. Before Christ's coming, Satan shackled humanity to death, deception, and wickedness. The Old Testament, though, largely anticipated the simultaneous defeat of physical and spiritual rulers. Even after Christ's death and resurrection, the disciples still ask him, "Lord, will you at this time restore the kingdom to Israel?" (Acts 1:6). The disciples have somewhat come to grips with the spiritual dimension of the kingdom, yet they are having difficulty in comprehending its future, physical dimension. At Christ's first coming, he initially vanquishes Satan's invisible kingdom but leaves the physical domain of earthly rulers intact. Only at his second coming, at the end of history, will Jesus fully conquer Satan and all earthly rulers and establish his kingdom in its fullness. All that Jesus initially fulfilled in his ministry will be consummately fulfilled in the new heavens and earth. Believers must grasp not only the nature of Christ's kingdom but also their participation in it. For example, we can be confident that when we suffer for the sake of Christ, we manifest the veritable presence of the kingdom. Just as Jesus ruled in the midst of suffering on the cross, we rule in the midst of our suffering.

One final comment on the nature of the kingdom is in order. The Old Testament generally expected that Israel's Messiah would be a descendant of David, an individual who would unite the tribes of Israel and bring the nations into subjection to Yahweh. The Old Testament also suggests that the Messiah would suffer, even die as he subdues the nations (e.g., Isa. 52:13–53:12; Dan. 9:26; Zech. 12:10). But Christ's messiahship differs in at least two ways: (1) Christ's rule (and his kingdom) is characterized by suffering. Indeed, when Christ and his followers suffer, they paradoxically and ironically manifest the kingdom. (2) Christ's rule includes a cosmic, divine dimension. Jesus does not simply govern the nations from Jerusalem; he rules over the entire cosmos from the very throne of the Father. He sits enthroned over the universe in the heavenly temple, surrounded by a myriad of angels and deceased saints. While the Old Testament hints at a divine Messiah (Ps. 110; Isa. 9:6; Dan. 7:13–14; Mic. 5:2), first-century Jews were not eagerly anticipating one.

Continuing in the vein of Christ's divine rule, the four Gospels do something rather remarkable: they identify Jesus *as* Yahweh. The Evangelists do not add Jesus to Yahweh, resulting in some form of bitheism (two gods); instead, they claim that Jesus *is* Yahweh. While Yahweh is one, there is a plurality within him. The church would work out the nuances of this in the following centuries, but all the ingredients of a robust Trinitarian theology are found in the Gospels. The implications for a proper reading of the Old Testament are astounding. If we identify Jesus as Israel's Lord in the Gospels, then every instance in the Old Testament where God is mentioned—which is everywhere (!)—we should include Jesus. In other words, when God acts and speaks in the Old Testament, we should also include Jesus acting and speaking. This line of thinking explains why Luke, without hesitation, depicts Christ stilling the storm, an act that only Israel's God can perform, or why the apostle John claims that the prophet Isaiah, in the well-known vision of Isaiah 6, "saw his [Jesus's] glory and spoke of him" (John 12:41).

Life in the New Creation

Believers not only participate in Christ's eternal kingdom but also enjoy life in the new creation. According to Genesis 1–2, God creates the cosmos to be his sanctuary, and while that sanctuary is deemed "good," there is an expectation that creation must reach a stage that exceeds its original state. The cosmos must be prepared to house the presence of God. If Adam and Eve and their progeny had obeyed God's commission (see Gen. 1:28; 2:15–17; 2:24), then humanity and creation would have achieved a state of glorification—that is, God would have transformed their bodies in a manner fit for the full presence of God. Creation, too, would have been transformed so that it could house God's glory. The fall ruptured God's relationship with humanity and creation. So God promises to send a Redeemer who will reconcile humanity to God and prepare creation for his glory. And when Old Testament prophets speak of a "new creation" or a "new heavens and a new earth" (e.g., Isa. 65:17; 66:22), they are referring to this consummate state of creation.

Luke taps into this theme of new creation when he invokes the new exodus theme and the year of jubilee (Luke 4:18–19). Like the already-and-not-yet nature of the kingdom, the new creation arrives in stages. Instead of God renewing the cosmos all at once, he does so incrementally but decisively in his Son. Jesus's life, death, and resurrection constitutes the "way" to the promised land of the new creation. Also, in his resurrected, glorified body, Jesus ascends to the Father's throne and is the first one to enter the heavenly promised land. On account of Christ's work, God plants those who trust in him, man or woman, rich or poor, Jew or Gentile, into the new creation. Believers are spiritually renewed and await Christ's return when God will fashion them into his Son's restored image. How can we as Christians today apply these insights to our daily lives? Though Christians still struggle with indwelling sin and will continue to do so until the resurrection, we must recognize our status as a new creation. The Spirit's presence in our hearts empowers us to conquer sin and please God in all of life. God also assures us that we have begun to participate in the new heavens and earth. Our life on this earth is tied to our future existence in the new eternal state. We should fall into the rhythm of the new creation here and now, so that when we arrive in the new heavens and earth, we will *continue* to love God and one another but in a greater, more profound way.

General Index

Scripture Index

The New Testament Theology Series

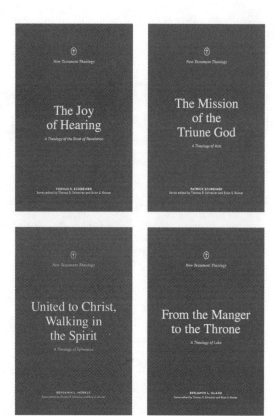

Edited by Thomas R. Schreiner and Brian S. Rosner, this series presents clear, scholarly overviews of the main theological themes of each book of the New Testament, examining what they reveal about God, Christ, and how they connect to the overarching biblical narrative.

For more information, visit **crossway.org**.